The

Ten Pound

Australian Pommie

by

Beryl Jackson

THE TEN POUND AUSTRALIAN POMMIE
BY
Beryl Jackson

Published by ABeFree Publishing 2022
ISBN 9781916310711

Copyright@BerylJackson2021

The right of Beryl Jackson to be identified as author of this work has been asserted by her in accordance with section 77 and 78 of the Copyright, designs and Patents Act 1988.

All rights reserved. No part of this publication may be reproduced, stored in a retrieval system, or transmitted in any form or by any means, electronic, mechanical, photocopying, recording, or otherwise, without the prior permission of the publishers.

Any person who commits any unauthorised act in relation to this publication may be liable to criminal prosecution and civil claims for damages.

Thanks to ABeFree Publishing for formatting the softback edition.
abefreepublishing@yahoo.com
http://www.buffry.org.uk/abefreepublishing.html

PUBLISHED

IN LOVING MEMORY OF

BERYL JACKSON RIP 2022

http://www/buffry.org.uk/abefreepublishing.html

THE TEN POUND AUSTRALIAN POMMIE
BY
BERYL JACKSON

CHAPTER ONE

The day we boarded the "Ellinis", it was cold, wet and dreary. I remember a reporter going up the gang plank with us, asking why we were leaving England; look at the weather I remember saying: "We haven't seen the sun in weeks - I'm going for some sunshine."

We were sailing on the £10 scheme, supported by the Australian government, as they were desperate to boost their population of Australia in the 60's. The "Ellinis" was full of immigrants, so much so, that men and women were separated, four men to a cabin and four women in other cabins. My husband was on a separate deck at the opposite side of the ship.

Our cabin steward showed us to our cabins, a lovely boy called "Gorgeo", who was to become a very good friend to us all by the end of the journey.

I was in cabin No. 169, sharing with Evelyn (whose husband was in my husband's cabin) and Meg, a Scottish nurse. I had my apprehensions about sharing a cabin, but I could not have chosen two nicer people if I'd chosen them myself. We were chatting and helping each other to feel more at ease in minutes, especially when the bed folded up to the wall with Evelyn still in it; we were in hysterics, I knew this was going to be a journey to remember.

We stored our luggage away then went on a tour of the ship. I felt quite at home on this ship. I loved her straight-away. Although small compared to some ships, she felt very big-hearted, warm and welcoming, all one class, which cuts out any snobbery and puts every passenger on equal footing.

We were lucky! We had an outside cabin and the deck led onto the swimming pool deck, with sun beds, a drinks and snack bar, bullion served at eleven o'clock, hot or cold, depending on the weather: hot of course while in the English port.

We met our husbands who were studying a plan of the ship; there's one on each deck as, although she's considered a small ship, she's still big enough for one to get lost and each corridor looks alike once you get away from the main rooms.

We headed for the morning room, where there was chamber music playing, very soothing and gentle, nice for a quiet drink and helpful to regaining one's equilibrium.

We set sail at 5 o'clock that afternoon, 31 July 1965. We went up on deck to wave goodbye to Southampton and England. I had asked my family not to stay 'til the ship sailed, as I knew it would have been too upsetting and I was right. People crying everywhere, it's a very big decision to leave family, friends and country, to make a new start 13,000 miles away. It's not a decision you make lightly, but once the ship leaves the dock, that's it, three blasts on the funnel and we are off.

Shortly after setting sail, the chimes sound for dinner. We are greeted at the dining room door by the two ship's captains. Yes, there were two on this trip, very pleasant good-looking Greeks, the "Ellinis" belongs to the Greek shipping line Chandris Lines. They welcomed us aboard and we were shown to our dining table.

There were about eight people to a table. The dining room was very big and very smart and clean, just like our table steward, another Gorgeo. We all introduced ourselves, then scanned the menu. What a menu! A welcome aboard meal with almost twelve courses. I don't remember what I had, but I do remember that every meal after that was just as well presented and nearly as many choices. That meal alone would have cost us ten pounds. We also got along fine with our dining room companions, we pool together for a bottle of dinner wine and decide we will do this every dinner 'till we reach Australia and we did. We went through the whole wine list and over, we toasted our journey and happy future in our new country. I was feeling very optimistic and thankful for having been given this amazing opportunity. Not only to start life in a new country, but a world cruise, four whole weeks, waited on hand and foot for ten pounds.

After dinner we headed off to the ballroom, where a Greek band was playing, but we are all too tired to dance, so we sat a while listening to really good dance music, then Eve, Meg and myself decide to have an early night, although Eve wasn't too happy. She had begun to feel seasick the minute the ship set sail; it took her quite a while to come to terms with the motion of the ship. Me, I slept like a log!

Breakfast was between eight and ten o'clock, I think I made it twice in the whole journey. I preferred to go to the snack bar on the swimming-pool deck for coffee and bullion, as I'm not a breakfast person. I'd meet my husband there and stroll around the decks, although it was still too chilly to linger for long outside, it would be quite a while before we could swim or sunbathe.

But, as soon as we entered the warm weather, the crew changed from black, warm, sombre uniform, to white, tropical, pleasant suits and the whole ship took on a very different face. The sun lounges came out on the decks, the swimming pool was filled up with water, children running and playing around, bathing costumes and trunks were rummaged out of the suitcases and everyone became more relaxed.

There were quite a few Australians on board, mostly students, who had been on a break from university studies. They were so laid back, it really helped us stiff upper lip English to relax and, having sailed out to England, they knew more about life on board ship. It didn't take them long to organise nightly parties that started when the ship's entertainment stopped for the night.

We would all put money in a kitty and buy a load of drinks for when the ship's bars closed. Then we would go out on the swimming pool deck and have a singsong, someone would bring a guitar, another an accordion, a mouth organ, drums. It was lovely, singing and dancing under the stars on those lovely balmy nights, until the passengers whose cabins were next to the deck, complained we were keeping their children awake, so the next night when we were in full swing, we had a visit from the Captains. They were very impressed by our little party and didn't want to spoil our nightly entertainment, so invited us to use the Captains' deck, in their private area. So each night we'd all troupe off up to the very top deck of the ship, away from the passengers' areas and sing and dance the night away.

We would have a Hawaiian night where we would all dress in Hawaiian dress, grass skirts, garlands of flowers, wrap around loincloths for the men, all made up of what we could improvise. We had Egyptian nights, Charleston nights and one night we had a Grecian night, togas made of bed sheets, wreaths for our heads made from bits of plants borrowed from the ship's display. We invited the ship's Captains, not dreaming they would come but, to our surprise and delight, they did and thoroughly enjoyed themselves. A couple of nights later Eve and I decided we would wash our hair and have an early night. That was the night Meg rushed into the cabin, shouting we'd been invited up to the Captains' quarters for a private cocktail party and me and Eve, hair wet and in rollers, missed out, but heard all about it next morning. They'd had a lovely time, but not as interesting as our parties.

Our first port of call was Los Palmas. The weather was glorious; we strolled around the streets in shorts and T-shirts. What a difference to England, to feel the sun on your body, instead of being stifled by layers and layers of clothes, trying to keep warm.

We went into a little coffee bar, we asked for coffee and were served with tiny cups of black coffee, so strong it nearly took the roof off your mouth. It was served with lumps of sugar; you put the sugar in your mouth, then slowly sip the coffee, till you got to a deposit of coffee grains that filled a third of the cup. It was horrible, to me especially, as I don't usually drink coffee, but we learnt by the passengers who had already been there, to ask for "café-au-lait". That way you got a glass with coffee and milk, which was quite nice.

I don't remember too much of Los Palmas, only that it was the first sunny country I'd visited in my life and how bright everything was and the people were very friendly.

We set sail from there in the evening, the sun was setting on the sea and everything felt warm and lazy and that's just what we did till we got to "Perizis", lazed about from morning till evening, except for meals. We spent all our time on the sun decks; we were golden brown in no time at all. Although the ship's doctor gave us lectures in the morning room, before reaching the hot weather, on how not to overdo it in the sun, some passengers ignored this advice and lots had to have treatment for sunburn. I took it slowly, about six minutes in the sun and half an hour in the shade, but I have the kind of skin that goes brown in the shade, so I didn't have any problems.

All the crew was looking forward to reaching Greece as they could all visit their families. Gorgeo, our cabin steward, came from Pireas and was looking forward to seeing his girlfriend, if only for a few hours. But when we disembarked he would not leave us until he'd seen us into his favourite taverna and bought we girls and our husbands massive Venice rolls full of everything you could possible get into a salad and ham roll and coffee and made sure the owner would take care of our every need, which he did.

We were staying in port till four o'clock next morning. By this time it was about four o'clock in the afternoon. We were sat outside the taverna when we decided to ask a family sitting at the table next to ours, if we had time to visit the "Acropolis". We had Gorgeo's translation book, so we tried to string a few Greek words together to form a sentence to ask the question. We were in stitches, as anyone who's ever seen Greek would know, it's not the easiest of languages, it took us quite some time. Then I plucked up the courage to try to explain to the family what we were trying to ask. I said in Greek, "excuse me," and in perfect English the lady said, "Yes, could I help you?" They all burst out laughing as, although they were Greek, they spoke and had understood every word we had been trying to translate. They advised us not to go to the Acropolis as it was quite a way from Pireas and we could not risk missing the sailing time.

So we got a bus into the next nearest town. I cannot remember the name, but we spent all evening there and, as there were quite a few of us, we decided we would get a taxi back to Pireas and the ship. We hailed a taxi, climbed in and were followed by a lad who was not in our party, a Greek boy. I said this is our taxi, you can't get in here, but was told this was the custom in Greece, if the taxi was going that way, it could fill up the taxi with passengers. Although I did a bit of arguing, as I thought we were full enough anyway, he refused to leave, so we set off. Meg had asked him how much it would be, from where we were to the docks and the taxi driver had given her a price, but halfway back, the taxi broke down miles away from anywhere. The taxi driver refused to call out another cab and insisted on the full fare. Meg was furious, but we paid up and thank God for our extra passenger. He was the only one who knew where we were. We walked miles back to Pireas and the boy took us right back to the docks. God knows what we would have done if he hadn't been with us. We were tucked up in bed by the time the ship sailed.

Our next port of call was Port Said. Eve and Fred, Sid and myself, went off on our own. It was so hot and phew, did it smell? Despite the heat, the Arab men wore lots of lovely wrap around woollen cloaks with hoods and the women (if you saw any) were all in very sombre black dresses and shawls. We were told before leaving the ship, to watch our wallets and handbags and trust no one, as there was always some passenger in trouble, each time the ship called here.

We were strolling down a street when confronted by this old man, who insisted on showing us how he transferred a coin from one hand to the other, without touching. I must say, I couldn't imagine how he did it, but my husband was not impressed. Just imagine how quickly he could whip your wallet he said and hurried us away.

We hadn't gone far, when we were followed by a group of beggar children, but we had been warned not to give them anything, as we would never get rid of them, not that giving or not giving made any difference, as we went into a bar to escape them, but they all waited outside. A Canadian in the bar said, "Are they annoying you?" He went outside and yelled, "Yaller" at them and they all ran off. He said, just shout "Yaller" and they'll leave you alone. We never did find out what yaller meant, but it worked, except for one little boy. He followed us everywhere. Poor little soul, he looked so pathetic, we decided as we'd been told not to give them money, we would give him some sweets. I'll never forget his face; he couldn't have looked any happier if we had given him money. He ran off, carrying the sweeties as if they were gold.

There was one experience in Port Said I will not forget. There were some lovely big palm trees all around a building with a very high wall and big imposing gates. These were the biggest palm trees I'd ever seen, so we decided we would have our photos taken by these trees. So Eve and Fred took Sid and myself and Sid took photos of Eve and Fred. We set off to walk down the road, when we heard footsteps running behind us and someone shouting frantically. We turned and, running towards us, were a couple of soldiers, bayonets on the ends of their guns, pointing straight at us. We stood petrified, not even understanding what they were saying, let alone what we had done.

There was a family walking across the road, who explained to us this was a military building and photos were prohibited, but we said we had only taken photos of the palm trees and thank goodness the family not only understood English, but had also seen us taking the photos. The soldiers said we would have to go back with them and wait till the photos had been developed, but by this time the ship would have sailed. We begged the family to explain to the soldiers we would be stranded if we weren't allowed to leave. They told the soldiers we were only taking photos of each other stood by the trees and they could vouch for that, as they were watching us and that if we were made to wait, we would miss the ship. Thank God, they believed them and let us go. We thanked the family and returned, shaking in our shoes, to the ship. Everyone had a story to tell back on board, but I think ours was the most frightening of all. By the time we went on deck next morning we were sailing down the Suez Canal. In fact, we heard we were the last ship allowed through, as it was about to be closed by Nassar and we were to call into Aden next stop, but the Captain got a cable from the British High Commission, advising us not to stop, because of the trouble, so we sailed on.

A couple of nights later we were to have a fancy dress party and parade, so some of us got together. Every night the crew lowered the ship's flag, which said "CHANDRIS LINES" from one deck onto a lower deck, then they would collect it, fold it up and take it away till they raise it again next morning.

So one night we hid behind the door leading onto the deck to which the flag was lowered, looking through the port hole and when the flag was lowered, a couple of the lads rushed out and picked it up, then we watched to see the crew members' faces when they came on the lower deck to collect it. They could not believe their eyes. There it was gone.

The Captain's face was a picture the night of the parade, when we walked in holding the flag aloft, "CHANDRIS LINES". One lad was dressed as the High Commissioner (no entry to Aden), another as a bar steward (what no Fosters?), another as a cabin steward (Tomorrow - as if they didn't want to be bothered they'd say "tomorrow"). I can't remember them all, but we did win first prize and the MC said the Captain says, can he have his flag back please? But all in good humour.

The next big party was the crossing of the line ceremony, "crossing the equator". This is the biggest day of all on board ship, when each passenger is initiated in the "solemn mysteries" of the sea.

Every passenger who wanted to be involved could be. The ladies were Mermaids of Neptune and men as helpers of Davey Jones. It all revolves around the swimming pool and it does help to swim, as at the end of the ceremony everyone is thrown into the pool.

On the big day there is an air of excitement around the ship, the sun is shining brilliantly, everyone rushing here and there, getting ready for the ceremony to begin. A Queen Neptune has already been chosen from the passengers. King Neptune is usually a member of the ship's entertainment party, along with Davey Jones. King Neptune has lots of mermaid helpers, fish and shells, all dressed in bright coloured crepe paper costumes, over swimming costumes and trunks. Davey Jones has pirates and sailors, all a motley crew.

After lunch we are told to assemble around the swimming pool, as the ceremony is about to begin. Neptune and his chosen Queen are sat already on thrones, waiting for their courtiers. When all the passengers are assembled, a trumpet blows and the fun begins. The courtiers drag reluctant passengers out of the crowd in front of King Neptune and accuse them of some trumped up charge. Like throwing empty bottles into the sea, Neptune gives the appropriate punishment, like "out with his kidneys". He is dragged, screaming, to a table, where a doctor and helpers are waiting. He is laid out on the table and the operation begins. There's red colouring for blood, very real looking fake forceps and the kidneys are a bunch of sausages. After these are removed, he is covered in flour and thrown into the pool.

By this time I had moved to a higher deck overlooking the swimming pool, as I can't swim and didn't want to be thrown in. More passengers were paraded in front of Neptune, Davey Jones speaks out in defence of the accused, not that it made any difference, as all had some part of their anatomy removed, covered in cooked cold spaghetti or flour, or both and into the swimming pool. At the end of the ceremony we are all handed a certificate to prove we are now honoured and respected members of Davey Jones and Neptune's Rex, Trusty Shellbacks and have been initiated into the "Solemn Mysteries of the Ancient Order of the Deep". We are then told there's a buffet laid out on one of the decks and believe me; I had never seen such a beautiful display of food created into exotic birds, fruit into animals of every description. Such a work of art, I'd never seen, it was truly a shame to touch it, but that was what it was there for, so we all tucked in.

That night there was a crossing of the line dance, with prizes for the happiest looking couple, the youngest dancers on the floor, spot waltzes and drawing your cabin number out of a hat. I must say here, that the Captains on the "Ellinis" on that trip really made her the happiest ship afloat, which wasn't always the case, as I was to find out on a later voyage.

And it wasn't all plain sailing, as we hit the tail end of a hurricane and had a few days of mass seasickness, crew and passengers. We had sides for our bunks which we were advised to use, it stopped you being thrown out during the night. We had very plain food to help prevent seasickness and told to stay indoors, under no circumstances to open the deck doors. Children had to be especially careful, parents were told not to let them run around.

Our little party got together and played cards, only poor Eve was ill out of us all and although I couldn't swim, I never felt frightened, I knew the little Ellinis would see us safely through and she did.

CHAPTER TWO

Our next port of call was Cape Town. Although we had newsletters and talks about every port of call before we arrived, we were not informed about apartheid. I still have the information sheet about Cape Town, about the history, the trading, who ruled it and when, but not one word about apartheid. But I felt the oppression when I arrived, not really knowing what it was, just that compared to the other countries we had visited, it felt sad and unhappy. What made it worse, it was Sunday and everything was closed, adding to the feeling of oppression. In the time we were there, I could not shake off this uneasy feeling, I knew it had nothing to do with the country itself, as it really is beautiful, with Table Mountain rising behind the city, surrounded by vineyards and sweeping down to sandy beaches. I cannot remember much about that first visit, what we did or where we went, only this feeling, of quiet sadness.

The next leg of the journey was quite long. The next stop was Australia. In the meantime, there was plenty to get involved in.

I enrolled to learn Greek dancing - two hours every morning - and I really enjoyed it. Their dancing is so expressive and one night the crew put on a real Greek dancing night. It was lovely, all dressed in their native costumes, a very enjoyable evening.

There was also bingo every afternoon, horse racing on the decks (wooden of course), croquet and keep fit.

There was also a gym where you could go any time and of course, the ship's entertainment every night. I can say I was never bored in the entire journey, it was just four weeks of absolute luxury for me.

Our first port of call in Australia was Fremantle, the Port of Perth. Some passengers disembarked here, as you were given a choice by the Australian authorities where you preferred to settle.

We went into Perth to have a look around and even then, it was a very lovely city. They say it's the only planned city in Australia. There are trees down the side of every street, "Fanjapany", "Acacia", each road lined with a different species of tree blazing in colour and the scent wafting the air. What struck me most was how clean everywhere was.

We went into a cafe for coffee and were surprised to find it was the same price as in England, in fact most of the items we saw were no more expensive than England. This cheered us, as the pessimists had said the cost of living was much higher than Britain. That's why the wages were higher, but we found this totally unfounded.

The people were friendly, very interested when we told them we were British migrants. We heard stories about how their families were the first settlers and how proud these people were of their origin and most of all, how proud they were of Australia and being Australian.

It was such as contrast from England, where no one seemed content with who he or she was, or what he or she had. We had left a very disillusioned Britain; it was very heartening to hear people speaking so highly of this our new country.

It wasn't too hot either that day as I remember a cool breeze blowing; everything felt idyllic.

We left Perth in the early hours of the morning; the next stop was Melbourne.

Before each port, films were shown about the area. We went to each one, as we wanted to learn as much about the whole of Australia as possible. We had chosen Sydney because we were told there were more work offers there than anywhere else in Australia. We had sailed a month earlier than planned, on the promise there would be someone waiting in Sydney docks with a job for my husband. It had been a great strain on us both but we thought it would be worth it to know we had a little security when we arrived.

Melbourne, how glad I was we hadn't decided on this city. All I remember of it was how distant and imposing it was, nothing about it welcoming or friendly, just large impersonal stately looking buildings, nothing about this city appealed to me at all, even the people were less friendly than Perth.

Next stop Sydney. I had very little sleep between Melbourne and Sydney, drawn between excitement and apprehension. We sailed into Sydney Harbour at night;

it was such a lovely sight, the bridge all lit up as if to say, welcome to your new home. It was a lovely balmy night, the feeling of apprehension overcome by a feeling of friendly welcome. We had to wait till morning to disembark; there was no sleep that night I can tell you.

The next morning we did go to breakfast, to say goodbye to all our shipmates and the crew. That was a sad moment. In the middle of the excitement, we had made some very good friends, but we all promised to keep in touch, except the crew of course, they would go on to more passengers, more ports. We tipped what we could afford, except for our cabin steward. We had clubbed together and bought him a little present. I think he was truly sorry to see us go.

But go we must. After a month of being in the bosom of the dear 'Ellinis' we set foot on Sydney's "Port Jackson". Luggage everywhere, we had to search for ours, among the thousands of cases strewn along the wharf. If I had any complaint about anything, it would be the way our luggage was discharged from the ship. We were lucky to find our cases all in one piece, but there were cases burst open, contents strewn everywhere. The luggage was rolled down a roller ladder, but it came so fast and furiously, that no one could move it away quick enough, hence burst cases everywhere.

We thanked God ours was still intact, then went off in search of our cabin trunks. They had also serviced the journey intact. We had to leave them at the docks, as we had no address at this moment, so we went in search of the man who was supposed to be waiting for us, with job and accommodation. But if he was there, we never found him and, as we had been found accommodation and booked on a bus to take us there, I wonder if he ever really existed.

As we didn't have children, we didn't qualify for hostel accommodation, so we climbed aboard a bus which was taking people to their destinations, temporary accommodation, from which we had to find our own permanent place to live.

By this time it was getting dark. I'll never forget that ride, the driver stopping in the dark, letting people off, explaining directions to which house or street was theirs and some of the areas were so sun-down I really began to feel nervous. People were dropped off here and there, till we were the only ones left on the bus. I asked the driver what the place was like that he was taking us. He assured us it was the nicest of them all and it was, "Concorde", a new suburban the outskirts of Sydney, ours was a new large bungalow, beautiful and clean, with a very nice landlady waiting to welcome us.

After a couple of days settling in, we started to look for work. We scanned the Sydney Morning Herald. It was full of situations vacant. Our landlady saw a diesel engineer required for Sydney Harbour Ferries. She insisted on making my husband an appointment for an interview, although he explained, he had never worked on marine engines. Her reply was, "Just don't tell them." So off he went the next day to a place called "Balmain", for his first job interview.

He was very nervous, not feeling too happy at the idea of lying. The manager was very open and friendly, he welcomed him to Australia and proceeded to show him around the ferries and explained what would be required of him. There, he introduced him to all the men and back to his office, at which point he asked if he'd ever worked on diesel marine engines before. This was the crucial moment, did he lie or tell the truth and risk not getting the job. He decided to tell the truth. "Well I respect your honesty," said the manager, "as you have told me the truth I will give you a go and I'm willing to teach you all I know if you are willing to learn." From which moment they became firm friends.

I found myself a job in the cafeteria of the "Pearl Insurance Company", run by an organisation called "The Worldwide Catering Company". The money was poor and the work was hard. There were only three of us - the cook, the manageress and myself. But in reality there were only two of us doing any work, the cook and myself. The manageress just walked around preening herself all day. I was also given the day's takings to take to the bank. I thought this was very trusting of them considering they hardly knew me but found out a few days later a girl had been attacked carrying her firm's takings to the same bank. After that, I carried the money in a brown paper bag.

We were only working in Sydney for a week when my husband's boss told him about a flat to let in Balmain, as Concorde was quite a way out of Sydney.

So we arranged to go and see it. It was a basement flat, quite big, scarcely furnished, owned by a lovely old lady who lived in the rest of the house with her deaf and dumb son. I liked her straight-away., she had a great sense of humour and very sprightly. The rent was more than reasonable, so we gave her the first week's rent there and then.

We moved in a couple of days later on a Sunday as my husband worked Saturdays. It was bedtime by the time we had got straightened out, so we climbed into the big double bed exhausted. I was just nodding off when I felt something bite me. I told myself it was just my imagination, but in a few seconds I was being eaten alive. I cried out and jumped out of bed, switched on the light, pulled back the bedclothes and found the bed full of fleas. This was my worse nightmare come true. I was in tears, my husband was so tired, he just said, "Get back into bed, you can't do anything about them now." But no way was I getting back in there. I sat all night on a wooden chair on the lino in the kitchen as they were also in the carpets. I cried all night, the next day my eyes were red and swollen. When I got to work the cook said, "My goodness girl what's wrong with you?" I burst into tears again and explained about the fleas. "Oh! Don't worry about that," she said, "just tell your landlady". But how could I tell her she's got fleas? Only dirty people have fleas in England but she explained that, because of the climate, fleas were to be expected. They lived in the warmth and getting the exterminators out to treat them didn't have the same stigma as in England. Maybe they had been lying dormant but when we moved in they had got active again.

I still could not tell our landlady. I had once worked as a nurse in a children's infectious hospital on a ward with cubicles and, when the children were moved out, we would tape up the windows and doors and use what was known as stoving powder to kill off any germs that may remain. You would just mix these two powders together and the fumes would fumigate the rooms, so my idea was if it killed off germs, surely it would be strong enough to kill fleas.

So on my way home I bought some from the chemist and some masking tape. We taped up the doors and windows and put some powder in a tin in each room, then went to sit in the park opposite the house. It wasn't till we stopped to think that we hoped we wouldn't kill off the old lady too. We waited for the two hours as directed, then went back and opened all the doors and windows. It nearly knocked us over, the fumes were so strong, surely the fleas must be dead now.

But not so. The minute I got into bed they started on me again. They didn't bother my husband so much as he was darker skin than me and he had also been in Malaya during the war and maybe built up immunity to them. But I was a mass of bites. I just couldn't stand it any longer, the next morning before work I knocked on our landlady's door, full of apprehension. How was I going to tell her she had fleas? But to my surprise and relief, she wasn't in the least offended. "Oh! I'll ring the exterminators right away, I'll see if I can get them here today". I could have hugged her; in fact I think I did. It was such a relief to have told her. If I had done that in the first instance, I could have saved myself a lot of

tears and trouble, as when we got home that night, the exterminators had been and we didn't see one single flea again in the year we were there.
Although one night we came very close to being exterminated ourselves.

One of my husband's work-mates was looking for somewhere to rent, as he had fallen out with his long term girlfriend and she had told him to leave and as it was her house, he didn't have any option.

There was another empty flat adjoining ours, so my husband asked our landlady if she would let it. She asked the man to go see her, which he did and he got the flat. He'd been there a couple of months, when one night I smelt gas. I got out of bed, checked all the gas points, the fire, the cooker, but couldn't find any escaping gas. I got back into bed, again being told by my husband, just go to sleep, but the smell of gas was getting stronger all the time. I got out of bed and found the strongest smell was coming through an adjoining door to the other flat, locked on the opposite side, so I crept outside and smelt under the other flat's outside door. The doorstep had a worn dip in the stone where people had stepped on over the years and, through this dip, the gas was seeping out. I rushed and woke my husband, dragged him outside and said, break the door down. After realising how strong the smell was, he broke open the door and there lying on the floor was my husband's work-mate. We dragged him outside into the fresh air, he was semi-conscious. We loosened his clothes and waited for him to come round. I made some tea, black and strong. My husband checked his flat for gas leaks, but found all the gas taps on the cooker, including the oven, turned on full. The man was very lucky, as it was only the dip in the doorstep that had saved his life. He had been lying opposite this flow of air. He said he could not remember anything, he had been out drinking and said he had turned the gas on to make a drink and couldn't remember anything else, but we knew it was more than that. Our landlady was woken up by my husband breaking the door, she had rushed down to see what was happening and was horrified as, if the guy had lit a match, we would have all been killed, blown to smithereens.

So she gave him notice to quit the flat the next day. It was all for the best as his girlfriend found out what had happened and rushed round to see if he was OK and then he moved back in with her.

My husband was very happy in his job, but I was looking for something else. I saw an advert for an assistant in the cafeteria of the Commonwealth Bank in Sydney, part-time, so as it was only in the next road from the Pearl Insurance, I went along there in my dinner hour. I liked the manager straight-away. My job would be working washing up machine, five hours a day, ten till 1 o'clock, one hour off for dinner. This also included dinner, anything on the menu, then one o'clock till three o'clock and nine pounds a week. I took the job, there and then, went straight back to the Pearl Insurance and handed in my notice. The next day there was someone from head office to see me. He said they had been planning to make me the manageress and he begged me to stay, but I had made up my mind, so I turned it down.

I was really glad I did too as I really loved my new job. There was less pressure and a great set of women to work with. One of the women lived in Balmain, so we travelled to work together on the bus, or by ferry.

She was married to a Scottish man, who had been in Australia since he was nineteen-years-old. He was now sixty-four. I went to visit them and even after all those years, he was still home sick. I remember him warning me, "It's a long way from home," but I was still fascinated by the newness of it all.

But I had to admit, as the days went by I began to feel very lonely as we had no real friends. Even the money began to feel less important. At first we were so thrilled; my husband's first week's wage was seventy two pounds, compared to fifteen pounds a week in Doncaster, England and my money was more part-time than I had been earning full time, but I remember one day saying, "I've never had so much money and I've never been so miserable."

CHAPTER THREE

One night after a night out in Sydney, we were driving home, when my husband suggested we could go to Brisbane to visit some very dear friends of ours, who had emigrated three years previous. "When?" I asked. "Tomorrow," was the reply. "You phone work and say I'm sick and I'll ring your work and say you are sick." So that was what we did. It wasn't a nice thing to do, but I was so desperate to see a familiar face, I would have done anything. The next day we were on the train to Brisbane.

Our friends didn't know we were in Australia and we had lost touch with them when they'd emigrated, but we had got their address from their parents before we left. Woodlands Avenue, Gails, Brisbane, we guessed it wouldn't be hard to find, but how wrong we were.

We had to get another train, from Brisbane, to Gails. The train stopped and we stepped off, into another world. The best I can describe it is, if you've seen those railway stations in the American westerns, where they step off the train and there's nothing, only a wooden hut and nothing else for miles, that was Gail's. We could not believe it; we looked up the road that was parallel with the rail tracks and the only thing we could see was a garage, way, way in the distance. The temperature was up in the nineties; the road was wavering in the heat. We each carried a suitcase and headed for the garage. It was afternoon, I realised what was meant by 'mad dogs and Englishmen'. I don't know how we made it, but we did, only to find the owner of the garage had never heard of Woodlands Avenue, or any other Avenue for that matter, but he did tell us there was a motel over the next hill so, after a cold drink, we struggled off to the motel. We booked in straight-away., as, by this time, all I wanted was shower and lie down.

After a rest we went to the restaurant, had a nice meal and began to feel much better. We asked the motel owner if she had any idea where Woodlands Avenue was. She had never heard of it either, but as we were talking, a taxi driver came in. I'll ask him, she said, he might know. He said he thought he did, but wasn't sure, but if we wanted to take the chance, he would take us there. So we set off through the bush, down a dirt track. It was beginning to get dark by this time, so all we could see was lights through the bush every half mile or so. We seemed to travel miles, before he pulled up outside a box on a post. "Nip out and see what number it says on that post", he said. Sure enough, it was the number we were looking for, but I doubted if it was the right house, as this house was set in two acres of lovely landscaped garden, sloping down to the road. The house was on the hill, beautiful, big French windows right across the whole of the front of the house, leading onto a large veranda. This couldn't be theirs, they'd only had a council house back in England and no money, plus three children. How could this be them, but, as we had come this far we thought we'd better make sure, so my husband and I cautiously walked up the path, then up the stairs to the veranda and knocked on the French door which immediately swung open and we were enveloped in loving open arms. I'll always remember that moment, it was good not only to have found them, but it brought home to me, just how much I'd missed a familiar face. Les had spotted us before we'd knocked, through a mirror on the wall opposite the door, he said he could not believe his eyes. When we said we had booked into a motel, he said, "No way are you staying there tonight, we'll go now and get your cases." So we paid and tipped the taxi driver, but for him we may never have found them, then Les drove us back to the motel to pick up our cases.

What a lot we had to tell each other and my, how the children had grown in three years, speaking fair-dinkum Australian, but looking so tanned and healthy. They all loved Australia, the children loved everything about it, even school.

We discovered that the following week they were going on holiday with their neighbours to the Gem Fields. David and Aileen were also English migrants and between them they persuaded us to go with them, not only that but Les and Jean suggested we pack up everything in Sydney and go live with them in Brisbane. We didn't need much persuading we were on the first available train back.

We handed in our notices to our work as well as our landlady, we didn't have time to work a week's notice, but everyone was very understanding when they knew we were going to be with friends.

It was a great rush to pack up and get back in time for the Gem fields. Our poor old landlady was very sorry to see us go and I must say I was sorry leaving her, as she had been very good to us over the year we'd been with her and I had grown very fond of her.

My husband bought a trailer for the back of the car and one of his work-mates, also English and his wife, came to help us pack. I wasn't sorry leaving the basement flat as seeing Les and Jean's house in Brisbane, it was more like I had imagined Australia to be. Sydney was nice, but it could be anywhere in England but for the sunshine. Everyone rushing here and there just like London, or any big city. I'd found the city of Brisbane to be a lot slower pace, more of a country city if there is such a thing. The people were friendlier and they had time for you.

I felt much more at home there, even the first visit made up my mind. I liked it there.

We arrived back in Brisbane the day before we were to leave for the Gem Fields.

Three weeks in the heart of the Australian bush, this was going to be very new to us. We had little idea of what we would need, but the others had plenty of experience, having bought and cleared their own two acres of bush before building their houses. We learnt how Dave and Aileen had helped Les and Jean clear and build as, having children, they needed a house quicker. Then Les, Jean and the children had cleared and helped build Dave and Aileen's house. We learned you could buy what is known as the apex and structure and build the house yourself. I could not believe they had done it all themselves, even the plumbing, although having no town's water, they only had an earth closet in the bush, other than that a house like that, only rich people had in England. They had worked hard, but what a reward. Each house standing in its own two acres of land.

So, prepared for anything, we set off early the next morning, for Emerald. Having already travelled from Sydney to Brisbane, we certainly did some travelling that week. We were in a convoy of three cars; Dave and Aileen, Les, Jean and children and my husband and myself. Everyone was very excited. We stopped after we were well on our way, at a bar-b-que area, these are like our picnic areas, only they have brick fireplaces with grills for cooking. The children went off to find wood, while we got the food together and in no time at all we were tucking into T-bone steaks and salad. In Australia, everything is accompanied by salad, even egg on toast or cheese on toast. People did appear to be much healthier, especially the children. Salad and fruit was the normal rather than the exception and when dining outside they took the perishables in a large plastic box called an 'esky', into which was placed the food, surrounded by packs of ice, when the ice melted there was a cap at the bottom of the box which you opened to let the water out, then you bought more ice at a machine that was installed in every garage. I have seen them in England recently, but Australia has had them for years. We also stopped at a garage for a shower; every garage also has a shower room. You placed ten cents in a slot in the door, walk in and take a shower and, believe me, after sitting in a car for miles and miles in ninety degrees, you really need one.

So, refreshed, we set off again. I don't know how long it took us to get to Emerald but I remember when we arrived, all we saw was a garage and a few houses, way in the middle of nowhere. This was where we had to fill up with petrol, as, from here on in, there was nothing, only bush. We bought loaves of bread and anything else we may run out of. After warnings from everyone we met to be careful, we set off into the Gem Fields for real.

One thing I remember clearly was the road in was all black mud and the cars were sliding everywhere. We were warned that if it rained while we were in there, we could be there for months, as we had to go through dry river beds, which turn into real rivers once it rains, but, undaunted, in we went.

Why they called them the Gem Fields, goodness only knows, as it's bush, bush and more bush. Very few people went there in those days, as it was considered too dangerous. We came to a little wooden hut where we had to leave our names and addresses and when we intended coming out and, if we weren't out by that day, they would come in looking for us to make sure we were all right.

We also had to take out a miner's licence, only a dollar, but if you did happen to find anything worth finding, that piece of paper allowed you to keep it, if not, you had to declare it and the government could claim it or part of it, but how anyone ever found out what you'd found, I don't know.

It was very interesting, just driving through the bush; every so often we'd come across a digger, living beneath a tarpaulin under a tree. We'd stop and have a chat and try to learn more about what we would be looking for. These people were so starved for company it was a pleasure for them to help you all they could. We would stay hours drinking Billy tea and learning about how they survived in the bush.

Most diggers never set up camp near their finds, as it was too obvious they had found something worth staying around for. They would camp a few miles away, so no one knew where it was but, after speaking to a few of them, it was obvious there were gems to be found and between themselves there was an unwritten law, no man trespassed on another's find, it was unscrupulous visitors they had to be afraid of, although in those days they were few and far between.

We found some of them were being paid by the government to stay in there and the government took a percentage of whatever they found but there again, how the government found out what they'd found, I don't know.

We were talking to one man, who said "look out for an English (Pommie) man, who lived in there, he's the one who's finding all the rocks". It seems he had struck it rich, so much so, he had moved his family, lock, stock and barrel, to live in the Gem Fields and we did find them. They were living in a small caravan with three small children. It seems they had been in Australia for four years when, like us, they had decided to be adventurous and taken a holiday looking for gems and he had found what was considered to be the best find up to that time, so they had decided to pack up and go live by their find. This was three years ago and now he was a millionaire. He would fly to South Africa to sell them and he must have felt safe enough with us, to show us some of his collection of cut and polished gems, set in beautiful velvet lined boxes. They alone must have been worth a small fortune. We set off in much higher spirits after meeting them. Who knows, we could be lucky and come out of there much richer than we went in.

Along with our miner's licence, we had been given a map showing where the wells were. We had to find one to camp close to, as we couldn't transport enough water for us all, so we chose one to head for. It was well into the bush and we had to drive through dry riverbeds to get there. Les and Jean's car kept getting stuck, as theirs was lower to the ground than ours or Dave and Aileen's and we had to keep digging them out. We found logs and branches to build ramps and to stop the wheels digging further into the mud, but it all added to the excitement.

We finally arrived at our chosen destination. We have bought an axe to clear an area to make camp. The others had brought tents, we didn't have one, not that I would have wanted to tent anyway with the snakes and deadly spiders, along with a thousand other creepy-crawlies to be found in the bush. The three cars were estate cars, so we slept in the back of ours on a mattress.

Lesley and I went to fetch water from the well; Lesley was Les & Jean's eldest son who was at college, he had studied all about gems and what they looked like, where to look and what to look for. There was a pile of dirt and pebbles near the well, so I picked up a stick and ran it up and down this pile of dirt and I swear to this day, this thing just fell into my hand, it didn't look like a pebble, or anything else I'd seen, not in the least like a gem as I'd imagined a gem to look like. "What's this Lesley?" I asked, holding it up to the sun. He nearly fell down the well with shock. "That's a sapphire" he shouted, "Auntie Beryl's found a sapphire". They all came running and we examined it closely, not that any of us knew for sure what it was, only Lesley was convinced he was right. How lucky if it was, I hadn't even had to dig for it, or even looked for that matter, it had just fallen into my open hand. I couldn't believe it, but I put it away safely till we could verify one way or the other.

There was no bucket in the well; we were lucky that Les and Jean had thought to bring one. We tied it to the rope and dropped it down and, as it hit the water, my what a smell! The water had become stagnant, when we drew it up; it was a horrible shade of green. We drew load after load, trying to skim off the top, but it wasn't getting any better, so we decided to keep all the water we'd brought for drinking and cooking and use the well water for washing only.

We went to bed when the sun went down, deciding we would be up at the break of dawn to make full use of the daylight hours. We were woken next morning by the calling of the kookaburras, a wonderful bird with an amazing group morning chorus. The others were used to them, living in the bush as they did, but my husband and I were experiencing the wonders of the Australian bush for the first time.

There's something very special about the bush, the knowledge that man has had nothing to do with its creation. It's there, as it was in the beginning, surviving up till now, as it was intended. There was a stillness I had not experienced anywhere before. I can't describe it well - a kind of holiness, that we all vowed we would honour while we stayed there. We would take from it only what we needed, not to destroy anything of its oneness. I don't know what I'm trying to describe here, but anyone who has ever got away from man, to God's creation, may understand. There's a knowing that we have lost in our rushing here and there, looking for goodness knows what. I'm sure an Australian Aborigine would know what I mean, but even he has had his way of life and his knowing taken from him by the pace of the white man. There's something here that words could never hand down to a younger generation, just a feeling, a feeling of familiarity, of being close to something you've lost and for which also you have the greatest respect.

And in that respect we set off, deciding not to go too far away from each other, we were to remain in calling distance of each other. My husband and myself stayed together, Les, Jean and children went off together, the children having been told, under no circumstances, to wander away from where Les and Jean could see them and Dave and Aileen took off in another direction. We agreed to leave some distance between us, but not too much.

My husband and I found a dried up stream; we walked along it, looking in its banks as gems like pebbles get washed into the banks when it's flowing. We were thrilled to find some small sapphires, but far too small to be cut and polished. In fact, most of what we found was small but the excitement of finding them was great.

We met up with the others for lunch. No one had found any rocks, but we were really enjoying ourselves.

We heard the sound of a car engine in the distance.

Who on earth could be out here we wondered, when this old broken down utility truck pulled up by the well, driven by an Aborigine. He had come for water. We told him it wasn't fit to drink, but were surprised to find he'd been drinking it for years. He lived in the bush on the money paid by the government to diggers. He had found one or two decent stones, but wasn't yet a millionaire, but here was someone who knew about gems, so I showed him my sapphire from the pebble heap. "Where did you get this?" he cried, "it's a beauty, a star sapphire". He held it up to the sun and pointed out the star shining inside it. I explained I'd found it in the heap by the well. "I know whose diggings that is", he said, "he'll cut his throat when he finds out what he's missed", but by law it was mine as he'd discarded the heap. What happens we found out was, if a digger isn't near water, he will fill up his truck with his diggings and take it to a well, where they riddle it with water, because the sun soon picks out a gem when it's wet, which this man proved to us. He put my sapphire into a riddle with some pebbles then poured water over them, the sapphire shone like the gem it is, soon distinguishing it from the pebbles. He handed it back to me, saying, "Take care of that, it's a beauty".

We were also able to do him a favour, as he told us he was very unhappy as he had lost his dog. He was driving along a particularly bad area and the truck had been bouncing about but he'd not checked to see if his dog was alright in the open back, as she had travelled with him for years, but when he'd got to where he was going, she was gone. He guessed she'd been shaken out of the van and injured. And he was right. As we were driving here we had met a farmer who lived on the outskirts of the Gem Fields who asked us if we found anyone who'd lost a dog would we tell them he had it. It had wandered, near to death, onto his property and he had taken it and nursed it better. He said she had a lovely nature and guessed someone would be missing her. The fellow was so excited and close to tears when we told him, he said he would go straight back to Emerald to collect her and was there anything he could get for us while he was there. We gave him money to get us more supplies, but after more than three days had gone by we guessed we'd never see him again. However, true to his word, he turned up bearing our supplies and his cherished dog. She was a lovely natured dog and very happy to be back with her owner. But no more than he was to have her back with him!

The three weeks we were in the bush seemed to fly by, but by the end we were running out of food anyway. The children had found their appetites out in the fresh air all day and had eaten Les and Jean's supply days before, so we pooled our resources. I remember making Yorkshire puddings with onions frying, big ones in a frying pan for us all and I think they were the best Yorkshire puddings I'd ever eaten. They were very filling.

We came back to camp one day to find the possums had rummaged through what was left of our food but, although it was strewn around, they hadn't found anything to their fancy. So I guess we were lucky. It was lovely at night round the campfire, looking up into the trees and seeing their big eyes looking down in curiosity. I realised they'd never seen anything like us before.

The day we were leaving we packed up all our gear, then decided we'd have a last search, so off we went in different direction. My husband found something that looked the entire world like a piece of black glass. We were on the point of throwing it away, when we realised, who could have thrown away a piece of black glass, the size of a fifty cent piece, way out here, so we decided to keep it, just in case.

By eleven o'clock on our seventeenth day we were all packed and ready to leave. We were all sorry to be going back, to so called civilisation. We made sure we left the area as we had found it. We took all our rubbish home with us, dug over the fire, so it would grow again, digging in the pot ash, as Dave and Les explained to myself and my husband who knew nothing about pot ash or anything else to do with the bush for that matter, but we were willing to learn.

Thank goodness it hadn't rained while we were in the bush, not that it was likely to, it hadn't rained there for about two years. Going out was easier than going in, as we'd learned a little about crossing dry river beds, we put logs and branches down before we got stuck and it worked.

We arrived at the little hut, much to the relief of the warden. He had had misgivings about letting a bunch of Pommies, including three children, loose in the Australian Bush, but for the fact that the others had lived in the Bush, I doubt he would have trusted us, as you read of so many English coming to grief going adventuring, without enough knowledge of the terrain. It was only the week before an English family had died trying to cross the Simpson Desert. I think the English are the biggest headache to the Australians, through not respecting the powers of nature to destroy as well as create. To nature it's abiding by the law, to us it's a matter of life or death.

We went into Emerald for petrol and a good meal. The garage owner asked if we had found anything, so we showed him our finds. We had one or two which he thought were decent stones, including my star sapphire, but we were most surprised to find he was more interested in my husband's bit of glass than anything else. He bought gems off the people in the Gem Fields, to stake them to stay there, he also had loads of cut and polished stones, set in velvet boxes and he also sold to South Africa, so we guessed he knew what it was, even if we didn't. So, if it's worth something to him, it was worth something to us. He asked my husband how much he wanted for it, but my husband said he didn't want to sell. He must have been pretty desperate, as he ran after the car as we pulled away, shouting he would give us anything we asked for it, but my husband decided not to sell.

CHAPTER FOUR

I realised after leaving the Gem Fields, how the fever grabbed the diggers, as the nine of us including the children were still searching every bit of area our eyes focused on. We walked everywhere with our heads down, searching, for weeks after, but this isn't as daft as it sounds around Emerald and Rubyvale, as the roads weren't all sealed at that time and some of the best stones were found lying in or along the banks of the road.

The road home ran parallel with the sea in some areas we travelled through and I'll never forget pulling off the road, driving through the bush to the loveliest beach I had ever seen. It stretched as far as the eye could see, miles of sun bleached sand and clear blue sea. I felt sure no one had ever been there before, only maybe the Aborigine, it was so pure and perfect.

We stayed long enough to have a swim and sunbathe. Then, reluctantly, we had to leave. We were all sorry we couldn't have pitched camp for a few days, but everyone was due back at work and the children back at school.

We arrived home, hot, tired, but happy, what a holiday to remember. The children couldn't wait to get to school to tell their friends of their adventure and show them the gems they'd found, it didn't matter that they weren't worth a lot of money, the adventure of finding them was worth more than money could buy.

We were made to feel so much at home by Les and Jean, they seemed genuinely glad to have us stay and this was confirmed when Dawn came home from school one day and asked Jean, "Have you told Auntie Beryl about that house?" "What house?" I asked. Jean explained she had told the children not to say anything, as she didn't want us to think she was trying to palm us off, but as Dawn said it anyway, she told us. Some friends of theirs were leaving Brisbane and they lived in a little bungalow by the gates of a disused industrial estate and they had asked Les and Jean if we would like it.

"Oh! That sounds lovely", I said. So we set off there and then to have a look at it, Jean assuring us not to take it if we didn't like it. But we did like it. It had a long lounge room and kitchen built in brick and the bedroom was built in a little courtyard, built of wood like a log cabin on small stilts. It was unusual to say the least, but very attractive and the rent was very reasonable. It stood in about twenty acres of land. There were big hangers where the Americans used to test their aeroplane engines during the war. A big six-foot wire fence with big gates, to which we would have the key, surrounded the land. There was one other house at the far end of the estate, it was occupied, but the people, who were leaving, said they hadn't spoken to them, they only waved, going in and out of the gate. Our bungalow had a lovely big garden and lawns. We were thrilled, how lucky to find such a place after only being in Brisbane for such a short time. We contacted the landlady and she agreed to us taking it, we moved in the day Les and Jean's friends left.

The first thing we did was get a dog, a pedigree German Shepherd pup. She was lovely; such a lovely nature and she loved us on sight, just as we loved her. We had no problem with her whatsoever, she settled in as if she had always lived there and the plus was the fence and the locked gate. I could let her out without worrying if she would wander off, not that she went very far without checking I was still there.

I had decided not to go to work, as I couldn't cope with the heat. I was happy to be able to stay at home, for the first time since leaving school. I had worked the ten years of married life, right up to the week before leaving England, but now, at long last, we could afford for me to stay at home.

My husband wasn't long in finding work at a place nearby, "Allied Interstate Transport". This firm transported goods from one state to another. The lorries were much bigger than any in England, but he liked it and the men he would be working with.

I enjoyed not having to rush around; I tell you living in a constant seventy to eighty degrees isn't as romantic as it sounds. It's all right for the Australians, they were born to it and if you have nothing to do all day, like on the ship, but working, travelling to and from work and cleaning and cooking, really took it out of me. Now, I could work at my own pace. I also enjoyed working in the garden, we made the place look as nice as possible. We had a visit from our now new landlady, Miss Mclye. She was very nice; we learnt her grandfather was a Captain Mclye, who had discovered Mclye and it was named after him. Most of the places in Australia are named after the people who discovered them. Balmain was named after a Captain Balmain. I loved to hear about the early settlers and the history of places, as the history wasn't that old that you couldn't relate to it. In fact for a new country, I was surprised how advanced it was.

We also got on waving terms with the couple from the other house, but as we only saw them coming and going through the gate in their car we didn't really have a chance to speak. How I wished I'd taken the initiative when one day they knocked on the door and asked if we would give their keys to the landlady as they were leaving. They had all their belongings on a trailer and were ready to drive away. It was only then we learned they also were English migrants and like us. They knew no one in Sydney and were very lonely, so they had decided to try their luck in Adelaide. They were such a nice couple and we all said we were sorry we hadn't spoken before and they said, "If we had known you, we probably wouldn't have left." But they did and we were sorry to see them go.

The house wasn't empty for long. This time we made an effort to be friendly with our new neighbours and how glad I was we did. They were Australians and they proved to be two of the best Australian friends we made in seven years. They also had a German shepherd dog, Duke and a little terrier called Candy. My German shepherd, Elsa, as we had called her, loved Duke on sight. They ran around barking joyously, having found someone to play with. He was a lovely nature and I soon learnt to love him too and we felt we'd known Ross and Zeena for ages.

Ross had a parcel delivery company and Zeena was a nurse, so we didn't see much of them in the day, but we would go to the drive-in cinema, at night, or to the swimming pool or the beach. Les and Jean were pretty restricted to what they could do, with having children, but Ross and Zeena, like us, had no ties. We would put the dogs in the cars and off we'd go.

One day Zeena came crying to our door. Ross had to go away and she couldn't afford to stay in the house on her own, so she'd got herself a flat. She could take Candy but not Duke. I begged my husband to let us have him, but he was worried, if he bred with Elsa, as she was a pedigree and Duke wasn't. He said "No, we are not having him and that's that!"

Zeena was taking him to the dogs' home the next day. I went to their house as soon as my husband left for work. "I'm going to take him Zeena, no matter what". I couldn't bear to let him go to the pound. She was in tears with relief.

That evening, just before my husband came home from work, I locked Duke in the laundry to give myself time to pluck up courage to tell him what I'd done. He drove in and Elsa went flying to the car as usual, making her usual welcome home fuss, then she ran barking to the laundry door, looking to him, then back to the laundry door. My husband said "You'd better let him out, I knew you'd never let him go to the dogs home". What a relief,

Duke shot out straight into my husband's arms, barking and crying, he knew he was here to stay.

We were happy in our bungalow but once Ross and Zeena left, we began to consider buying our own place, with a lot of encouragement from Les and Jean. Les said he would help us all he could if we did what they had done and buy a shell home, so we began scouring the papers for land for sale.

One evening my husband said "this sounds good, shell home for sale standing on four acres of land, three thousand dollars", which in amounted to one thousand five hundred pounds. "Never", I said, "they've made a mistake", but we rang up the next day and sure enough, that was the price, but we were to find out why when we eventually found it. It was out in the bush; we were given directions where to find it, but after three attempts searching every dirt road in the area, the agent met us and even after him losing his way two or three times, we found it, but there was little wonder we'd missed it. All there was to see was a white surveyor's stick in the middle of nowhere, with No 36 on it and a small path cleared through the trees and at the end of that path, a small house, hidden from the road.

What a shock, shell home, this meant there was no inside walls (although it could have been worse, Les & Jean's hadn't even outside walls when they started), no nothing, no plumbing, no electric, no towns water, concrete floor, no dividing walls, no sink, no bath, just nothing but the outside walls and roof and a 2,000 gallon water tank outside the back door to catch the rain water off the roof and that was our water supply.

The agent was a Hungarian migrant, a very nice guy; he laughed when I asked, "How do we live without electricity?"

How green we must have appeared to him. "The best way you can", was his reply. It seems they had built this house as an experiment, thinking if there was something with a roof over their head, people would be more encouraged to live in the bush. It only takes one enterprising couple to start, then others would follow, as the land around us had been sold, all in four acre blocks, but our house had stood empty for four years, as no one wanted to be trail blazers.

But how could we miss such a bargain. Les and Jean gave us the last bit of encouragement we needed, so we bought it. It was only forty miles away from my husband's work, which is nothing, in Australian terms, that's on the doorstep.

So we gave our notice on the bungalow and moved in. I'd never realised before how much I had taken for granted. The first shock was turning the tap on the water tank to find to our horror it was empty, eighty degrees and no water, but the Gods must have been smiling on us as at that moment an old van drew up in the land and this old couple walked towards the house. Who on earth could this be, way out here? "We saw you moving in", they said, "and we are your neighbours, we live about four miles down the road and we wondered if there was anything we could do to help?" I thanked God for the Australian hospitality, how lovely of them. We explained the water situation. "Oh! We'll soon sort that out," said the lady. "Joe, you go fetch a couple of churns of water and ring the council to fetch 2,000 gallons on Monday". She explained you could buy water from the council, 16 dollars (£8) per 2,000 gallons. It didn't take Joe very long to return with the water and I made tea on a Primus stove. We sat on packing cases, happy to find we were not entirely alone out here and over the years they proved to be very good friends. We did find out Joe was English, he came here as a boy, living in foster homes if I remember rightly. He was around sixty but didn't know his real age, as he had no birth certificate.

The next day was Sunday. We were still English enough to want our Sunday dinner but how do you cook without a cooker? As we found out, necessity is the mother of invention!

My husband found a wire shelf, so we propped it up on bricks, dug a hole underneath it, cleared around it and built a fire. I put the chicken in a tray covered with foil, put the veg in the pressure cooker and placed them on the fire and I swear that was the best roast chicken I've ever eaten, although you have to be very careful not to start a bush fire.

That's why the first priority was to clear the bush around the house. We bought two axes and cleared what is called tea-tree, but it's nearly impossible to get rid of, as you're clearing it, it's growing up again behind you.

The only light we had for a while was a lead from the car but one morning the battery was flat. However, true to Australian hospitality, someone stopped with jump leads and saved the day. That night my husband came home with a paraffin lamp, kerosene as it's known in Australia. Really it was a lovely thing; it would have been considered an antique in England. We also purchased a paraffin fridge, I had never heard of such a thing, but it worked wonderfully. You put paraffin in a little tank like in a stove, light the wick, push it back under the fridge and lo and behold the fridge starts to freeze up. In fact, it worked better than any electric fridge, being twice as big and the top shelves were freezers, the bottom shelves just cold. It proved its weight in gold.

We bought a Calor gas cooker, although we had to be careful we didn't run out of gas as no one would deliver way out there, but even to this day, there's no way of telling how much gas there is in a cylinder till it's run out, so we had to revert back to our outside cooker more than once.

The dogs loved their new home and how glad I was of their company. I didn't feel in the least bit frightened out there on my own, as I know Duke would have defended me to his last breath. Elsa believed she who barks and runs away lives to bark another day, but they were lovely company.

We found out from Joe and his wife that there was a mail delivery. The mail man would also deliver bread or any other groceries, if you let him know what you wanted the day before. This guy owned the only store for miles, besides being the post office. He stocked everything but he didn't deliver to the door, only the end of the drive, as some drives were miles long.

We put up a large mailbox, which would hold bread or anything else we may run out of. The first morning I left a note for bread and bacon, but to my horror when I collected it, both bread and bacon were running with ants, so I threw both away. "Oh! You shouldn't have done that", said Joe's wife, when I told her. "Just open the bread (you'd wonder how they got into a sealed loaf in the first place) and they'll all disappear and wash them off the bacon, it will be alright. Don't throw it away and what you need", she advised, "is an old fridge to stand at the end of the drive, these are sealed and less likely to be invaded". So that's why there were fridges left on the roadside every so often, I had wondered. Well you would wouldn't you?

We had been given the plans of the house by the agent, but the plan showed that the already existing building was to be divided into kitchen, bathroom and living room but, as we had four acres of land on which to extend, we decided to have one large kitchen come dining room. We had already divided the bedrooms and there was one room built on to the house, the laundry, where the dogs slept.

We called the house "Tudor Cottage", a little bit of England out in the Australian Bush. We put up black beams along the ceiling and we bought "burnie board" (I don't know what they'd call it in England) with a design I swear was a Tudor Rose. We lined the inside walls with this. Les and Jean came when they could to help and advise. Les helped put in big casement windows that looked out on to the four acres of bush, which one day I hoped would be paddocks and lawns. They installed a large double sink and plumbing leading to a sump they had dug out down the bush. My husband put in cupboards and a breakfast bar; everything was done in black and white and looked very effective.

We purchased a lovely dining room table and chairs from friends of Ross and Zeena. These also would have been antiques in England and there wasn't a mark on them. The table was mahogany and it took two people to lift it and six chairs. I was so thrilled, we put lino on the floor and eventually carpeted, although as it got dark at seven o'clock in summer and four o'clock in winter, it took longer than we had thought, as we just couldn't turn the light on when it got dark, we had to leave whatever it was we were doing. The pity of it was it got light every morning by half past three. A lot of wasted daylight, although some people suggested we get up then and do whatever needed doing. Why on earth they didn't introduce daylight saving I failed to understand. I wrote to a daily paper suggesting this and they got an overwhelming response in agreement and I was surprised to find the following year they altered the clocks to get one extra hour's daylight, although Zeena always moaned about going to work an hour early.

Sometimes if the lorries broke down in another state my husband had to go there and occasionally had to spend the night away. These nights I would leave Duke loose outside and have Elsa indoors with me. I also had a sawn off shotgun by my bed. "You'd never use that", my friends would say. "Don't ever try me out", I warned.

My husband had made friends with another English migrant, John. He came to visit us, with his wife and two lovely little girls. I liked Hazel straight-away. and the girls were such a pleasure to have around.

John helped my husband to clear the bush. They first cleared a path all around the four acres, which wasn't easy, as all they had for guidelines was an occasional white surveyor's stick, but they did it and at last we could walk around our own land. It felt good, I couldn't believe how big four acres was, as the land ran lengthways into the bush, which was good, as we only paid rates on the land running parallel to the road that was about an acre across. In those days the rates were only twenty one pounds a year.

One Saturday John arrived all raring to go, they had planned to clear all the bush from around the house, as on one side the bush came up to the house. They had cleared a good area on the other sides, but my husband wasn't feeling too good and was lying down. "Oh, come on", I said, "John's come all this way to help, couldn't you at least try". So he made an effort and they really did well that day. They had cleared all the bush well away from the house by the evening and how lucky we were that they had, as next day was nearly one hundred degrees Fahrenheit. It felt very oppressive and like the lull before a storm, all morning I felt uneasy. It's strange how I felt something was going to happen and, sure enough, a car came flying up the road, squealed to a stop outside, men shouting, there was a bush fire heading this way. We were to fasten in the dogs, close the windows and doors against flying sparks and try to contain it as much as we could away from the house. I heard the fire before I saw it, a great roaring sound. I hadn't thought about a bush fire having a sound, but of course it had. The sky was bright red and it was roaring towards us, like a great red monster. We had the only tools available for fighting a bush fire at that time, a long strong stick with a piece of old car tyre nailed to it. So, armed with these, we waited. God, how lucky we were that we had cleared so far around the house, as when the fire reached us we were able to beat it out as it crept along the short grass. Except, of course, the bush we hadn't cleared, but that didn't matter as it was well away from the house. The fire just roared through there. There's nothing we could have done to stop it anyway. The heat was intense and the smoke choking, but we managed to keep the fire under control and well away from the house, but it was very frightening as it was burning all around us, even across the road; fires can jump across wide motorways, so it was inevitable it would jump our old dirt track. So we were surrounded. It's amazing how quickly a bush fire moves as in no time it had roared through our land and on up the road and we could do nothing but watch.

After a while a fire engine pulled up, they shouted, asking if we were all right. We said that we were, so they roared off. Without a town's water I suppose they were limited to what they could do. It's mostly a case of beating out the bush where there's no access to water.

Later we got a call from the police; they were going all around the roads checking on everyone. They told us two houses had been destroyed and if we hadn't cleared the bush, our house would have most likely caught fire. They said how they wished everyone had cleared around their homes like us. We gave a silent prayer of thanks to John, but for him we could have lost everything. We were told to keep an eye out for snakes now, as they couldn't get into their holes in the ground because it was too hot.

The next day after my husband left for work, I climbed back into bed exhausted, to be woken later by Elsa whining. I woke up and saw her heckles standing up on her back, she was whining and staring above my head. I looked and there all along the headboard was a snake. I shot out of bed, like a bat out of hell and ran behind a partition in the next bedroom. I had been warned, not to take your eyes off a snake, as they could curl up anywhere, so I poked my head around the partition and each time I looked it looked at me. After a while it slid on to my pillow, then down on to the floor. I kept hold of Elsa and waited. After about half an hour, it slid back on to the bed, up on to the headboard and out of the windows. I nearly fainted in relief.

When I was relating my frightening experience to John and my husband that night, I stretched out my arms, saying, "it was this big". John pulled in my arms and said, jokingly, "How big, Beryl?" suggesting that I was exaggerating. "It was a fair dinkum Aussie snake", I told them but I know they didn't believe me. Next morning Elsa spotted it again. It was curled around the two thousand-gallon water tank and the tank was outside the back door, its head was between the wall and the tank. There was no way I could get back into the house, but at that moment I heard a car coming up the lane. I ran out shouting and waving my hands and to my relief it was John. "You know that little snake I told you about? Well it's back! It's curled around the water tank", I said, "and I can't get back into the house". "Let's have a look", he said bravely, but his face want pale when he saw it. "GOSH! You're right, it is a fair dinkum Aussie snake", he said. "I told you it was", I said. I told him the gun was by the bed, so he dashed through the door and out again with the gun. He pointed it at the snake's head. He said, "it's either your wall, your water tank, or the snake" and pulled the trigger and shot the snake straight through the head. He held it up proudly, "shall we cut it up for the Kookaburras?" he said. "No leave it over the fence so my husband can see it" and when my husband came home, I said "you know that little snake I told you about, well come and have a look".

He couldn't believe his eyes and the next day we had screen windows and doors fitted so you could leave them open, but nothing could get in, not to protect me I don't think, but make sure he never had the same experience.

CHAPTER FIVE

We worked hard on the land and after the fire, grass grew better, we were told, it wasn't unknown for unscrupulous people to set fire to the bush deliberately, so the grass would grow thicker and better, but what kind of idiot would do that I couldn't imagine. I would spend most of my days chopping and clearing tea-tree and the smaller trees. We found we could get poison from the Forestry Commission free, to poison the roots as you chopped them down, so we got some and it worked. What we cleared stayed cleared and grass started to grow. We left the lovely big gum trees, despite being told by the Aussies, "You'll never get grass where trees grow". Who told them this goodness-only-knows but every property we'd seen owned by Australians was completely bare of trees.

Our grass grew lush and green. We had many a stranger stop and ask how we had managed to get our land so good, but I worked every day digging up grass from lush patches and placing it in sparse patches. We used our own fertiliser, as having no town's water; we had no flush toilet, what was known as an "E.C.". I'd scanned the papers in Sydney wondering what "E.C. for sale" meant. What on earth was an E.C.? It turned out to mean "earth closet" but it had its advantages. We would dig it into the land and I swear this was why our land was so good.

Then we acquired our Lucky. Les and Ralph, also English migrants, started their own business turning wood stoves into oil. They would go out to the big ranches and sheep stations. One trip was to a Merino stud farm in a place called Longreach. As they were driving back through the property in 100 degrees they found this baby lamb that had just been born, all on its own, no shade and as they thought was about to die, so they picked it up and put it in the van and stopped at the nearest place to buy milk. They dipped the end of a towel in the bottle and tried to get the lamb to suck it, but it wasn't interested, so they squashed a tin together, put milk in the tin and Ralph stood with the tin between his legs, while Les pushed the lamb from behind to where the milk was dripping out and it started to drink. We were curled up laughing when they told us, Ralph stood there, milk running down his legs, it must have been a sight to see. Anyway, they intended to keep this lamb alive and they did.

When they got him home, Jean and Dawn took it in turns to get up in the night and bottle-feed him. It soon became apparent he was quite a little character and whoever said sheep are stupid couldn't have been more wrong where he was concerned. He would play with Jean's two Maltese terriers and have them running round in circles, but one day Jean came home to find something had bitten his ear. We didn't think it was one of her dogs, but a neighbour's bigger dogs and as Jean was working and couldn't keep an eye on him all day, she asked if we would like him. I was over the moon, as I'd fallen in love with him the moment I saw him. My husband built a pen for him. When we collected him, we put him in a sack with his head out the top thinking he'd be alright till we got him home, but halfway home I felt a nose on the back of my neck. I turned round and there he was, stood on the back seat, looking out of the window as if he did this run every day. It was fun to see the faces of the drivers in the other cars; they couldn't believe their eyes.

We fastened the dogs up before we took him out of the car. I still wasn't sure how they would be with him. We put him in the pen, then let them out. They rushed over to the pen. Elsa took one look and walked away, as if to say, is that all the fuss was about, but Duke was quivering in excitement, crying and whining, running round the pen trying to reach him. "Well," I said, "there's only one way to find out if he wants to play with him or eat him." So I lifted Lucky out of the pen and put him down in front of Duke. He was so gentle with him; he gently smelt him all over, then licked him and immediately took him under his wing. Lucky wasn't worried as he'd been around dogs all his little life, so it seemed the feeling was mutual, as Lucky went bounding after Duke and they were playing like old friends. I breathed a sigh of relief.

I let the dogs and the lamb out the next morning, watched for a little while to make sure they were all right, then went about my chores. About an hour later I went out and neither lamb nor dogs were anywhere to be found. Oh my goodness, had I put too much trust in the dogs, my mind ran wild, had they taken him into the bush and at this minute were making a meal of him? I ran off down the bush, to come to a clearing and there they were Elsa and Duke lying together with the lamb snuggled between them. I'll never forget that sight (the lion and the lamb shall lie down together). I just wished I'd had a camera with me, what a picture.

After that I knew I had nothing to worry about and Lucky thrived. It was such a pleasure to see him and the dogs playing together. He'd bounce around them, then go gambling off, but they were always so gentle with him and he was so funny and as I have said, so intelligent. He'd nip a few of my plants occasionally, but after a few tellings-off, he learnt they were not for eating, but he would slowly munch his way towards them, then look up to the window to see if I was watching, if he didn't see me, he would much away quickly, but if he saw me watching, he'd bounce away as if to say, I wasn't going to touch them, honestly.

One day, in ninety degrees, he was so hot that his fur was thick and curly and he just stood in one spot panting. So I rang the vet to ask if he knew anyone who would shear him. "I could", he replied, "if I can keep the wool for my fee". "Done!" I said. I was happy with this arrangement so the vet collected him; on his trailer he had a wire cage which Lucky was very happy to travel in. He just stood there looking around as they drove off down the drive. He was a good and gentle vet that we'd had for the dogs so I trusted him.

He brought him back a couple of hours later. I could not believe it, he looked all the world like a skinned rabbit. He knew he looked strange, as he went into the laundry and stood in a corner. After saying goodbye to the vet, I found the dogs stood on either side of him. I swear they were laughing at him and he was looking so sorry for himself. I ushered the dogs out, took him in my arms and loved him, he snuggled his head under my chin and I said, "you'll be a lot cooler now and I still love you".

Anyone seeing me would have thought I was mad, but I knew he understood. I gently took him outside, told the dogs not to laugh at him and they also understood and Duke licked him as if to say, "We're sorry," and they went off playing happily. But I think that was the first time Lucky realised he wasn't a dog!

There were times Duke disappeared for two or three days, we didn't worry after the first time as he came back OK, but one time he didn't come back. Two, three, four days went by and by the fifth day I was beginning to worry. I rang all the pounds within our area, asked the milk, mail man, if he'd seen him or heard anything of him. No one in our area had seen him. When it got to the tenth day I was sick with worry. I was sat in the kitchen crying, my husband said, "You'd better begin to accept he's never coming back". When I looked up, there he was looking through the screen door. I rushed over shouting "He's here, he's here!" I put my arms around him, crying my eyes out in relief; he just flopped on the floor, exhausted. He looked so thin and weak. He drank a bowl of milk but didn't eat any food. And he made it clear to Elsa that he just wanted to rest as he growled gently as she made a fuss. He lay asleep all that day and all night. I was convinced someone had taken him away and he had found his way home. He ate a large bowl of food next morning and seemed so much better but the minute we took our eyes off him he was gone again. "That's it", I said, "I'm not going to worry about him any more" and I didn't. He returned three days later, looking very smug, so we guessed he'd been after a bitch in season and by the look on his face, it had been worth it.

A few months later I was working on the land when in the distance I saw a man carrying something down the lane. I called my husband, as no one ever walks in that heat, but as he approached we saw he had three puppies in his arms. "Have you seen a puppy anywhere?" he asked, "I gave some away and the bitch has carried the rest into the bush, I've been all day looking, I've found these three, but there's one still missing. At that moment Duke bounded round the house. "That's the father to them", he said, "I had my bitch fastened in for ten days while he was around, but let her out a couple of days when he disappeared, then he came back and surprised us, he lulled us into a false sense of security".

Duke seemed to know, as he stood there looking on proudly. I explained he'd come home on the tenth day and how worried we'd been. "Well, if you hear of anyone finding a pup will you let me know", he explained he lived about ten miles down the road, we said we would, but I didn't think he'd ever see it again.
The next morning as I was saying goodbye to my husband I thought I heard a whimper. "Turn off the car engine a minute" I said, "I'm sure I heard a puppy cry". "Oh! It's your imagination", he said, but did as I asked and sure enough there was a faint whimper coming from the long grass opposite the gates of the drive. I ran down the drive, across the road, bent down and this

little wet bundle of fluff jumped into my arms, snuggled in whimpering. "It's the puppy!" I shouted. Duke and Elsa came to see what the fuss was about and Duke went made, bounding around barking and trying to get at the pup. I carried him into the house, put him down and Duke rolled him over, licked his bottom and his face just like a bitch would have done. He was over the moon with him. The pup seemed to know Duke was his father as he soon stopped crying and wandered around smelling for food. He found Duke's dish and tucked in. Duke just stood by proudly watching him. My husband said "We can't take him back now or I'll be late for work. We'll take him back tonight."

So I had the pleasure of his company for the day. I say that as it was so lovely to see him playing with Duke and Elsa and he was such a confident little thing. Once he'd recovered from his ordeal and after a play, he curled up under the cooker and went to sleep. I had to fasten Duke and Elsa outside so he could get some rest, but they sat by the screen door, not wanting to let him out of their sight.

When my husband came home from work, we put the pup in the car and returned him to his owners. They were so pleased to see him. "He's promised to friends of ours", they said. I felt a slight tinge of sadness as we left him.

Next morning as my husband was getting into the car, I thought I heard a whimper again. This time my husband was convinced it was my imagination. "But listen!" I said. Sure enough, there it was again. I ran down the drive and there in the exact spot, was the puppy. I could not believe my eyes, how had he got here again? He surely couldn't find it himself. We guessed the bitch must have carried him back. I said "I bet she's saying to our Duke, you look after him". "Well, he's not", my husband said, "two's more than enough, we are not having any more, we'll take him back again tonight".

So Duke, Elsa, Lucky and myself played with him all day. He was such a lovely little character; we all fell in love with him. When my husband came home, I said, "can we keep him, he must have been meant for us, as the mother keeps bringing him back?" "No! And that's definite" he said, "no way".

So we put him in the car again. I was very quiet as we drove him home. "Alright" said my husband, "if they say we can have him, we'll keep him". I was so happy, I sent up a silent prayer, please let us keep him.

The couple were very pleased to see him, yet again. "Can't we keep him?" I asked. "The bitch seems like she knows where she wants him to be and as owners of the sire, we should be allowed pick of the litter". "Well, he is promised", they said, "but you are right, the mother must have carried him over there again, so guess she trusts you, so if she's chosen you, I suppose we can't go back on her decision". I hugged them in relief and picked up the pup and made to leave before they changed their minds. The pup snuggled up in my arms in the car, he knew he was going home.

On my birthday, my husband came home from work looking very secretive. "Close the doors and don't come out till I tell you", he said. So I went indoors and waited. I heard a very strange sound, but couldn't for the life of me guess what it was. "It's alright, you can come and look now," he called.

I went over to the pen where he stood and there were two baby calves. "Oh! How lovely" I cried, hugging and kissing him. They were lovely, only one had its bottom jaw protruding. "What's wrong with its mouth?" I asked.

"Well, I went with every intention of only buying one" my husband said, "but he looked so pathetic I asked what was wrong with it and the woman said they were going to kill it the next day, so I bought him as well". "Oh! I'm so glad you did, poor thing", he was a little bull calve and the other a heifer. I climbed into the pen and gave them both a hug. Daisy, as I called her, wasn't that interested, but Fred, as I called him, was so sweet. He snuggled up and let me love him and that's how it continued, Daisy being very independent and Fred being very loving and gentle. I had to bucket feed them and Fred was still sucking on my fingers two years later. He was a darling; I'd never known a gentler animal.

We got busy clearing and fencing, so we could let them out into a paddock. The first day was a pleasure to see they ran around kicking up their heels in delight.

But we also had to hand feed them as we were going through a dry patch. We read an advert in the local paper for Lucerne, so one night we went over to find it.

It was getting dark by the time we did find it, but a very pleasant young man came out to serve us. It was a small holding, with animals wandering around in the yard, one was a mare and foal. My husband fell in love with the foal, "I don't suppose you want to sell it?" he asked. "Well", said the boy, "I have a few horses and I love them all, but with the drought my father says I've got to sell some, so maybe I will sell it. The mare is in foal again, so they'll have to be parted soon".

My husband was delighted; he had always wanted a horse, so we arranged for the lad to bring her over at the weekend. He rode them through the bush, the foal following the mare. They arrived early in the morning, but the lad took one look at the paddock. "You'll never keep the foal in there", he said. We must have seemed so green to him. Of course we should have known the foal wasn't going to be separated from its mother so easily, or the mare from her foal. "You'll need a round yard", he said. We'd never even heard of one before. So we left the mare and foal in the paddock while we decided what to do over a cup of tea.

"I don't suppose you'll sell us the mare as well?" asked my husband. The lad thought a while. "Well, I have two mares in foal and I was waiting to see what they have, as I don't want a stallion. If I knew they were both having fillies there'd be no problem, but I suppose as they are here now, I'll have to take that risk. Yes I'll sell you the mare as well and keep my fingers crossed. Belle, which was the name of the mare, should foal in seven months". He even knew to the day. We discovered the best time to mate a mare is immediately after foaling. So there we were not one, but two horses and another on the way.

We were wondering what to call the foal next day, when I was doing my hair. I had a hairspray called Tania. "I know", I said, "let's call her Tania". "Yes!" my husband agreed, "that's nice", so Tania it was.

The dogs loved the horses on sight, especially Duke. He loved everything, there was always room in his heart for anything we turned up with and the horses were no trouble as long as they were together. Belle was a very good mother and watched over Tania, but we knew we were going to have to part them before the new foal was born, so we set about building a round yard, or a holding yard as it is otherwise known.

We chopped down some of the smaller trees, my husband dug post holes and we placed in the tree trunks in a circle, placing other tree trunks across from post to post. We built it about seven foot high, it was certainly very strong and sturdy when finished. How I was dreading putting Tania in there, fearing she would go frantic and hurt herself, as we'd been told some foals do.

So the day came; we decided the best thing to do was to put Belle in there with her to start with, just till she got used to it. We put some Lucerne in there, then led them both in. Belle wasn't worried in the least, it was obvious she'd been in a round yard before and Tania wasn't worried, as her mother was quite accepting the situation. She just walked around smelling and nibbling the wood but soon got bored and went over to her mother and started eating the Lucerne. What a relief, no worries what so ever. I was sure it's mostly the lack of concern for the feelings of the animal that creates fear and distrust. I am now more sure, most traumas in animals could be avoided if only humans took more care and gave more thought on how to make it less fearful for them.

We could eventually put Lucerne in the round yard and Tania would go in of her own accord. We'd gently close the gate, talking to her all the time and as Belle was wandering around where she could see her, she just settled. We didn't leave her in for very long to start with, but eventually we could take Belle for a ride without her even knowing she'd gone. We had broken her away from her mother with no distress at all.

When it got nearer the date for the foal to be born, we contacted the vet in case of complications. The last few nights I'd be out of bed racing down the paddock at the least sound but the night she was born we didn't hear a sound. Belle did it all on her own. We went over to see everything was all right and there was the most beautiful animal I'd ever seen. She was a golden brown and so beautifully proportioned, tall with long racehorse legs on which she was staggering around, still unsteady, but not in the least bit afraid. I stroked her gently with tears streaming from my eyes, what a precious moment; Belle looked on full of pride. I let the dogs out, saying to Duke "come and see what we've got". He followed me to the paddock, saw the foal and I'll never forget the look of pure joy that shone from his face. He looked at her, then at me, in sheer delight. I said, "be gentle". He went over and sniffed her and then licked and licked her. She smelt him, nuzzled him and Belle looked on, knowing here was yet another member of Duke's loving family. He never left her side all day, even when Belle wanted to feed her. In the end I said "come on, she's Belle's baby, not yours, leave her alone with her for a while". The other animals just accepted there was another member to the family, no big deal. Duke's adoration of Cindy, as we called the foal, never waned. He adored her.

By this time we had cleared and fenced another paddock for Tania. We'd put her in there, the fence running between her and Belle's paddock. She also adored her sister on sight; Belle would stand by the fence, letting the two foals nuzzle each other, she really was an amazing mother, very proud and protective of both foals.

CHAPTER SIX

The next thing was to get Tania broken in. There was a ranch on the corner of our road owned by a guy called Butch. He had about thirty horses and ran Dude Ranch weekends for visiting ships to Brisbane. We asked him if he knew anyone who broke in horses and he said he did. It was so near, we decided we would let him do it, so my husband led her there early one morning, I didn't go, as I didn't want to see her fear of being left somewhere strange. My husband assured me she'd been all right when he left her. Butch had put her in his round yard, with some feed. She was there a couple of days when it started to rain and not rain like we get in England, tropical torrential rain! The next day I felt apprehensive. I'm sure that out in the bush senses we haven't felt in years reawaken. Not only did I feel it but Belle was very jumpy too, running around her paddock, calling and neighing. Within the hour she was frantic, snorting till her nose bled, calling and looking at me to say, "do something". I said to my husband "something's wrong with Tania, go to Butchers, see how she is". He roared off in the car, to return half an hour later leading a very sorry looking Tania. She was covered in mud with blood and grazes on her stomach; her eyes were filled with fear. "My God!" I said, "what happened to her?" "Well", said my husband, "Butch was riding her, breaking her in, in the round yard, when she slipped in the mud with her legs just under the round yard and they couldn't get her out". "What! You mean to tell me they were trying to break her in, in all this mud, no wonder she fell". "She's alright", he assured me, and "she's only scratched". "And scared to death." I said,

"She's not going back there again". I led her to Belle who neighed and nuzzled her, so relieved to have her back. I felt so sorry I'd let them both down but I swore no one else was taking them where I couldn't see what was happening. I sponged her down, loved her and said I was really sorry and I would never let anyone hurt her again.

So how were we going to get her broken in as my husband and I weren't good enough riders to do it, when this young boy who often stopped as he was out riding to admire our horses, especially Tania, came by and noticed Tania's grazes. "What happened?" he asked. My husband told him. "Oh! What a shame", he said, "I've broken in my own horses and never hurt them, would you trust me to try?" "Only if you do it here", I said, "I'm not letting her out of my sight again and you are sure you know what you are doing?" "I promise", he said.

So we arranged for him to come then next day. He arrived early, he firstly fed her for us, stroked and talked to her, gaining her confidence. He just got to know her for a few days and her to trust him. She liked him and we trusted him, as his horse adored him, nudging and nuzzling him all the time. I never once saw him lose his temper; he just spoke very gently and reassuringly to Tania all the time. Within a fortnight he was riding her around the paddock, no traumas, distress, or fear, saddle, bit and rider fitting together like hand and glove. In fact, Tania was enjoying it as much as Kenny, which was the boy's name. He loved her, said she was a lovely ride. He was so proud of her and came every day to ride her and Belle looked on as proud as a mother could be.

In the meantime we also acquired "Suzy", a goat in kid. We were passing by a smallholding one day, with a sign outside saying 'goat for sale'. "Oh, wouldn't it be nice to have goats and have our own source of milk?" I asked my husband. "Alright", he said, "we'll see how much they want for it". I think we paid ten dollars for her, but she was worth much more than that, by the fun she gave us over the years, she was the funniest animal I'd known, a real character, from the moment I saw her I loved her. She never did give birth (I said we were the ones who'd been kidded), but she was just fat and contented and would eat just about anything, especially onion peel. I'd never known any animal eat onion peel, but she loved it. Like everything else in the family, she just fitted in, no trouble.

It was hard work looking after the animals and clearing bush, especially in eighty to ninety degrees and I had begun to feel dizzy and short of breath, but I put it down to the heat. I developed a rash on my upper arms and my tongue was very red and sore and the dizzy, faint feelings got more regular. I went to the nearest doctor, who mis-diagnosed my symptoms and sent me to a gynaecologist, who sent me for a small operation. I went private and here I must say, the treatment I received there was terrible and the standard of hygiene was even worse, but I was told later, had I gone public I would have received much better treatment. Anyway I was discharged and told to return in ten weeks time for a check up.

Was I glad to be home. My husband collected me in the utility van. When we pulled up by the side of the house, Elsa went mad when she saw me and jumped straight through the open van window, crying and licking me to death, with the other two running and jumping around frantically. What a welcome home! I had only been away two weeks, but being fastened in four walls, it was like being let out of prison, just to see the sky, the trees and my lovely animals,

I remember saying to my husband, "I pray I will never take all I have been given for granted". The horses neighed happily when they saw me; I loved and stroked them. What beautiful animals horses are, so proud and yet so gentle when treated with love and affection. The goat also showed her affection by running around in circles and bleating like crazy, as I said what a homecoming. I did my rounds, loving and saying hello to them all, but then had to go back to bed, as I still felt very weak.

Dick and Jim came to see me, I remember Jim saying "Gosh! You look so pale, you must take it steady and get some colour back in those cheeks". As I've said Jim was a male nurse, so I guess he looked upon me as a patient, as well as a friend. I think even then he was surprised as how ill I looked, considering it was supposed to be a very simple operation.

My husband went back to work after a week. Dick and Jim were very good, they helped with the animals all they could and I just potted around, but after about four weeks I still wasn't getting my strength back, in fact I felt so much weaker and couldn't stand up without feeling weak and dizzy and it was at this time I got this terrible longing for home. I suppose it felt like a child feels when ill, only the arms of its mother are going to be of any comfort. I longed to see the green fields and country lanes again, familiar faces and family. I remember saying to my husband, "if I die, don't bury me in Australia, promise you'll send me home". "Don't be silly, you're not going to die", he said. But I didn't seem to be getting any better and the homesickness got worse.

One morning, after I'd lay crying most of the night, my husband returned. He hadn't gone to work. "You can stop crying", he said "I've booked you on the Ellenis. You're going home. I've left it an open ticket; you can come back or if you decide you want to stay, you can ring me and I'll sell up and come home. And I'm taking you to another doctor tonight". He had done all this without saying a single word about it. I was overjoyed, I couldn't believe it, and I was sailing for dear old England in three weeks time.

That night he took me to a village doctor out in the bush, Dr Shellshear, of Beenliegh. I have put his name and the name of the village, as I have to thank this man for my life, I remember going into his surgery and feeling so weak and feeble, I just burst into tears. He was lovely. "Just sit there and tell me all about it", he said gently. "Well, I don't think I can carry on much longer", I remembered saying, then told him about my dizziness and going for the operation and how I felt weaker instead of stronger by the day. He gave me lots of confidence to tell him exactly how I felt, then he said, "did they give you a blood test before they operated on you?" When I thought about it I couldn't remember anyone giving me a blood test. "You mean to tell me they operated on you and never gave you a blood test?"

I was positive they hadn't, I'm sure I would have remembered if they had. So he turned to my husband sand said, "you must take her into Brisbane tomorrow to the place where they test the blood, I'll give you a letter to take. That way we can get the results back quicker".

So next day I went to have a blood test, but slowly this nagging thought went through my mind, what if it's something that's going to stop you getting on that ship? I couldn't bear the thought, so the night I was supposed to go for the results, I wouldn't go. "Nothing's stopping me getting on that ship, I argued," with my husband, "I'll be alright once I'm on the ship."

We went to play cards with Dick and Jim a couple of nights later. "What were the results of your blood test?" Jim asked. "She won't go to find out", my husband said. "No! Well I'm going to ring the doctor now", said Jim, which he did, before I could say a word, on which the doctor said for my husband to get me in the car and go out there straight-away., although it was long past surgery hours. When we arrived he said, "you know when you said you couldn't carry on much longer? Well in the condition your blood is in, I would say you would have lived another two weeks at the most, you have Pernicious Anaemia and more than likely that's what you've had from the very beginning. It's a wonder you recovered from the operation at all, your blood is so thin". At which he gave me a Cytamyn injection. "How long will I have to have these for?" I asked. "For the rest of your life young lady", he replied and I still remember just minutes after the injection I began to feel life was coming back into my body, thanks to this wonderful doctor, although by this stage I weighed only six and a half stone, my pallor was yellow and I must have looked terrible. He asked me about the medical history of my family and he was convinced by what I told him about the death of my mother and eldest sister they had most likely died of pernicious anaemia. I knew also my youngest sister had been very ill while I'd been in Australia. I remember getting the letter from dad saying she had been very close to death, but a woman doctor in the Norfolk and Norwich Hospital had saved her life. I had sat and cried, feeling so helpless, being so far away, little did I know that at that very moment I too was going to nearly die of the same thing, as later I found it was also pernicious anaemia.

Doctor Shellshear said it was hereditary so all my family should get blood tests. I wrote home straight-away., but my family was rubbished by the English doctors saying it was nonsense to say pernicious anaemia was hereditary. What a shock I got when I got home at the attitude of the English doctors, but Doctor Shellshear gave me a letter for the doctor on the ship and enough injections to last me for 6 months weekly injections of Cytamen 1,000 mcg, so it wasn't going to stop me getting on the ship after all (but I could have seen Bishops Rock then died).

Jim was so pleased when we got back, he said, you've got colour in your cheeks for the first time in months, I thanked him for ringing the doctor, how stupid I had been.

CHAPTER SEVEN

I had to go to Sydney to catch the ship as big passenger liners didn't dock at Brisbane at that time, so we called to pick up Les and Jean on the way and they came to see me off, plus I was laden with photos for Betty and Ralph's family, which I had promised to go and see, plus get Joe's birth certificate from Somerset House, if possible, as he was sure he'd reached pension age, but couldn't get it without his birth certificate. I also promised to see if I could find any of his family, he had had no contact with them since arriving in Australia.

It was a big thing, sailing twelve thousand miles on the Ellenis, going aboard without knowing a soul, but I felt such an affection for this shop she looked just as splendid moored in Sydney as I remembered her. But, once aboard, I realised I'd forgotten how big a ship is, even one considered not too big like the Ellenis, but I was given my cabin number and shown to my cabin by a steward, accompanied by my husband, Les and Jean. They were allowed on the ship till sailing time. My cabin was on 'D' Deck, the bottom deck. I was to share with four others, as this was the cheapest way to travel. I was the first to arrive so I chose a top bunk, as I thought better than being disturbed by anyone climbing up the ladder late at night. One girl arrived as I was putting my luggage away, she seemed very nice, if the others were as nice as she was and this could be a very pleasant journey. Then Les and Jean, my husband and myself went for a tour of the ship. It was like being enveloped in the arms of an old friend. We had a drink at the bar then went on deck. I was worried about leaving my husband to go to work and care for the animals, but Kenny had promised to ride the horses for us and Dick and Jim said they'd do anything they could to help, plus Ross and Zeena and Mr & Mrs Helliwell (Joe and wife), so we were very lucky to have made such good friends.

The call came over the ship 'will all visitors please now leave the ship'. This was the big moment; from now on I'd be alone. I kissed my husband goodbye, kissed and hugged Les and Jean, waved goodbye as they walked down the gangplank. I had asked them not to wait till the ship sailed as it could be ages and it only made leaving worse, so I made my way back to my cabin, glad to see that the girl was still there. She was feeling as lost as myself, so we went up to the lounge and had a drink. She was Australian going on holiday to England.

We went out on deck, when the three blasts from the funnels announced we were ready to sail. It's a funny feeling, sailing away from a familiar shore. There was sadness and happiness mixed up inside of me, as I wasn't sure I would ever see Australia again. Would England be the same as I remembered her? Or would I be on the first ship back. Well, even if I had glorified everything I'd remembered of her, the cruise was just what I needed to recuperate, so I was going to sit back and relax and enjoy myself.

Jude and I found our way back to our cabin to find the other girls had arrived. There was Jude, myself, Penny and Susan, they seemed really nice, and we were chatting away in no time. Jude was going on holiday, Penny was going to appear in T.V. commercials, Susan was travelling with her boyfriend to visit their parents' relatives and tour the continent. I was the only English person, so it wasn't long before they were asking me all about England, how long I'd been in Australia and why was I going home. I told them about my illness and how homesick I'd become. They were very sympathetic and from that moment on really looked after me. But now when I look at my passport photo I thought I must have looked like I'd just come out of Belsen. I weighed barely six stone, my eyes were all puffy and I was jaundice yellow. But, true to Australian spirit and although I was sick and at least ten-years-older than them, I immediately became one of the girls. I really enjoyed their company, especially after being out in the bush for five years, hardly seeing a soul; it was lovely having such good company for four weeks.

The chimes went for dinner. We were not at the same dining table, which is a good policy as you get to meet more passengers that way. I can't remember much of my dining room friends, but they must have been friendly or I guess I would remember them.

The day after setting sail, I had to go for my injection to the ship's surgery. I gave my letter to the doctor who also said "you are a very lucky lady, I'll see you every two days, see how you are coping". He was so kind, I felt better already and also our cabin steward, who was an elderly gentleman, took special care of me. He would bring me fruit and a tray at night with a hot drink and biscuits. The girls would pull my leg, but I think my husband had tipped him and asked him to keep an eye on me.

I was so lucky on my journeys as my travelling companions were as nice as I could have chosen for myself.

Our first port of call was Tahiti. By this time we had made friends with Alf and his son, John. I think John fancied Jude, but it was too late, she had already made friends with one of the ship's musicians, yet another Gorgio, but he seemed to be smitten with her too, as I must say she was a very lovely looking girl and also very sweet. Anyway the three girls, John and myself decided we would see Tahiti together. We were disappointed when we arrived as we found we were seven miles away from the beaches and being Sunday, everything was closed. We decided we would take a taxi to the beach, so Jude who could speak French, asked a lady who was working behind some big wrought iron gates in what looked like a garage, where we could get a taxi. She asked where we wanted to go. Jude said: "To the beach!" She asked us to wait. We thought she had gone to ring for us a taxi but no, she had fetched a car and pulled up and told us to get in. We didn't know if this was a taxi, but after seven miles we reached the beach. She refused to take any money but wished us a lovely day and a good journey to England.

How I feel sorry sometimes when I see how the English treat our tourists as every country I've ever visited, I've known nothing but kindness.

We spent the day on the beach; the sand was nearly black, it was very strange sitting on black sand, it was due to volcanic eruptions over the years. Funny how we take so much for granted, I have never even thought that all sand wouldn't be brown, golden, or even nearly white, but black, never.

Tahiti really is beautiful and the people so lovely, but the humidity is so high I found it far too hot, but there were coconut trees growing on the beaches, so I stayed in the shade while the others swam and sun bathed. We ate at a nearby snack bar and were surprised at how reasonably priced everything was; it was a relief to us all, as we were all travelling on a shoestring. As it got dusk we got a taxi back to the port. The ship sailed at midnight; we went on deck to watch the lovely lights of Tahiti disappear into the night, we'd had a lovely day.

I really can't remember much of the other ports of call, but I do remember we hit the tail end of a hurricane. It was worse than the one we'd experienced on the Ellenis before, but I trusted her to see us through and she did, but the captain and the crew seemed to care little about the passengers on this trip, it was a different captain and the crew seemed very unhappy and subdued all through the journey, so when things got tough, like during the hurricane, they just gave up on the passengers altogether, which wasn't very reassuring, but we had seen very little of the captain all through the journey and what we had seen of him wasn't very impressive. He was ruling this ship with a rod of iron. There were two very heavy officers next in charge and you would have thought they were running a prison-ship. As I said earlier, the Ellenis definitely wasn't the happiest ship afloat that trip. I wrote a letter to the captain saying so, as the atmosphere starts at the top. It was such a shame and it wasn't fair to the passengers or the crew but, true to form, that little ship saw us safely through. We found from the crew that was the worst weather the Ellenis had ever encountered, how I loved that ship.

I had Christmas and New Year on the ship, so I guess it was early January when we arrived in England. I remember thinking everywhere looked dark and damp, but the joy of seeing my family again after six years compensated for the weather. My nieces and nephews were no longer babies, my father looked older than I'd imagined he would be, but he had met a new lady he was hoping to marry, so he was very happy. I stayed with my sister in a Yorkshire mining village, she was married with two children and I was so thrilled to see children still played in the streets. I remember saying, "That's one thing I've missed, the sound of children playing." "I wish they'd go and play somewhere else", was my sister's reply.

I realised more and more all the things we take for granted that we turn the taps on and out comes water.

After six years of watching every drop, I had the compulsion to turn off taps left running, even bath taps, as we had only had showers to save water and oh, the pleasure of sitting on a proper toilet! And no worries of red back spiders under the seat!

And buses! I remember just arriving at the bus stop in time to watch the bus disappearing around the corner. "Damn!" said my sister, "Now we have to wait for the next one". "How long will that be?" I asked. "Another twenty minutes", she replied. "Linda", I said, "I haven't seen a bus near my home in six years." I swore at that moment if ever I did come back to England to live I would never get into the habit of complaining about everything and that I would not take everything for granted. I thought that was one thing living in the bush had taught me.

I really enjoyed my six months holiday, I visited Betty's mother, who naturally had a little weep as she looked at the photos of the grandson she hadn't seen, but I was able to reassure her that Betty, Ralph and baby were very happy and doing very well.

I found Joe's family by advertising in a Manchester paper, where he came from. They were lovely people and very glad to hear Joe was still alive. I managed to get his birth certificate; he was just sixty-five-years old and old enough for the pension, so there was no worry there. I met Joe's niece and nephew, who I heard later, had gone out to Australia and stayed with Joe and family.

I visited all my relations and my husband's. Everyone was so pleased to see me and wanting to know all about Australia. Why on earth should I want to come home to live after achieving so much in so little time? It was the question I was beginning to ask myself. Nothing seemed to have changed, everyone seemed just the way they were when I'd left, I was still shocked at the standard of living, the poor wages and the price of everything, everyone was still penny pinching. What I had taken for granted was the money, after six years of no money worries, I had thought things surely must have improved, but they were just the same. I had all this to take into consideration. Did I want to spend the rest of my life penny pinching, or staying in Australia and being the proud owner of a house and four acres of land? Another two years and we would own it, lock, stock and barrel. Had I got what it would take to leave all my lovely animals behind which I loved so dearly? Could I live inside four walls again, after the great Australian space? I had felt so shut in since being home as; being winter, all the doors and windows were kept tightly shut. I remember going out one night to stand on the lawn to get some air and look up at the stars. "What are you doing out there?" my sister asked, "you'll get your death of cold".

One night my husband rang from Australia. He had found a buyer for our place, what did I want him to do? I had to let him know in a week. Did I want to stay in England or go back to Australia? Now was the big decision time. I know I missed most the sunshine, everywhere seemed so dark and grey, I also missed the bright colours of Australia, the bright clothes, everyone in England seemed to have only two colours, black and grey, maybe an occasional brown. Also the houses were painted in such dismal colours, whereas in Australia, with a mixture of so many nationalities, the houses were painted in bright light blues, greens, reds, purples, no two houses were the same. Was my longing for England just in my mind? Did I really want to give up all I owned, for what would maybe turn out to be a big mistake? After a lot of thought and consideration, I sent my husband a telegram: "DON'T SELL LOVE BERYL".

After having made the decision, I felt ready to go home again. It was as if I had been waiting for something to make me make up my mind. So I booked on the Chandris Lines 'Australis', one of the biggest passenger liners afloat. I said goodbye to my family and travelled to Southampton alone. This is how I wanted it, but I remember travelling on the train, I sat there with tears streaming down my face, looking at the lovely countryside, it was now April and the grey and brown was slowly being replaced by blankets of green, buds appearing on the trees, the days getting longer, the sun beginning to shine more often, the faces of my family so fresh in my mind. How I was going to miss them.

This was the time I didn't go on deck to watch the ship leave port, I felt I couldn't bear to say goodbye to England for the last time, I was still being torn between my love for the two countries, but I told myself, I'll be alright once I'm home.

'Australis' - this ship was lovely, the Pride of Chandris Lines' ships, as I've said, one of the biggest passenger liners afloat in those days. I was sharing a cabin with a mother and daughter, they were very nice and friendly, they were going to Australia for the first time, to live with the eldest daughter and husband, who were sponsoring them, although the mother had met and got engaged to another passenger before reaching Australia. I often wonder what happened to all the people I've met on my travels, we were like ships that pass in the night, but I would not have missed meeting any one of them.

Everything about this ship was commendable. Lovely cabins, spotlessly clean everywhere, smart clean crew, beautiful food, served with a smile, good entertainment, very nice, pleasant captain. There was nothing, in the whole of the journey, to complain about - 'A1' in my book.

We called at the same ports I'd been to before, but no less interesting. I made a lot of friends in no time. There's nothing I've found more relaxing than a cruise for making friends, you can forget there even is an existence, beyond this beautiful floating haven. I could have happily stayed on the 'Australia' sailing the seas to the end of my life, but of course it was back to reality once we reached Australia. Even on the first port of call, I think I knew, although it wasn't a conscious decision, that this wasn't my home. I felt it was like visiting an old and trusted friend, who does all in their power to make you feel at home, but one day you know you are going to have to go home.

It hit me the most in Freemantle. The sun was shining like white light, my eyes hurt, even with sunglasses. The heat was overpowering, everything was too much trouble. I remember Kathy, the little girl from my cabin, asked her mum, "Can we go back to the ship, I feel sick?"

I didn't feel too great myself so we went back to the air conditioning of the 'Australis'.

I'll be all right once I get home, I told myself, I'll soon get used to the heat again and the sun shining every day, the flies and mozzies. I was longing to see my husband and animals again.

We arrived in Sydney in the early morning, I searched the faces of the crowd gathered on the docks and there he was waving frantically, along with our very dear friend, Ross. They had driven all the way from Brisbane to meet me. I rushed back to my cabin to gather my things and say goodbye and good luck to Kathy and her mother. We hugged and swore to write and then I went to join a very large queue waiting to disembark. Before I knew it, I was in my husband's arms, tears streamed down our faces, Ross joining in and how happy I was to see them again. They collected my suitcases, stowed them away in the back of the car and we were away. I waved goodbye to the 'Australis', wishing her in my heart very safe journeys where ever she sailed on the seven seas.

There was so much to tell, but first, I wanted to know, were all the animals all right. "Don't worry", said my husband, "we've managed fine. But we have all missed you". After a few miles, I fell asleep, what with the heat and being awake most of the night before. I slept nearly the whole journey home.

From here on, I can't really say what happened, I think my mind must have blocked it out. I can't remember arriving home, or seeing my animals again after six long months. I feel I was frozen in time, not daring to allow myself to feel, as deep down I knew, I had to go home, the heat started to affect my health again, I didn't have the energy to attend to the animals, or clear the land and shortly after arriving home we had a cyclone. What it didn't blow away, it washed away, I think that day was the day I made my final decision, I had to go home.

My husband saw I was slowly losing any health I had regained, so one day he asked, "would you like us to sell up and go home for good?" "What about the animals?" I asked. "You are more important than the animals", he replied, "we'll find good homes for them all, don't worry". "Alright" I said, as by then I knew, although everything I loved was here, my heart was back home in England, the pull was even stronger than before.

So we advertised the property and set about finding homes for the animals. No problem where Duke was concerned, Ross and Zeena would be over the moon to have him back and Duke went crazy over them each time he saw them. I must admit here, it was going to be harder leaving him than any other of my beloved animals, he was not just a lovely dog, he was a lovely soul, and I thanked God he could go home again.

We had made friends with some other English migrants. He did a security round with his beautiful German Shepherd dog. He had once said to us that he wished he could find a good bitch to buy as most of the dogs he'd seen looked scruffy and underfed. He'd also told us a stray mongrel had wandered onto their land and he and his wife had taken it in and cared for it. So I knew they were good-hearted people. So I approached him about Elsa, he said he would come and look at her. So he came over that night and they fell for each other. Elsa loved him and he could not believe how lovely she was and such a sweet nature. "When can I take her?" he said. "Well it's best to get the hurt over as quickly as possible, so I guess you should take her now". "Lovely" he said, "how much do you want for her?" "Nothing" I said, just as long as you take very good care of her and give her lots of love". "I'll certainly do that" he promised. We went out to the van where I handed over her pedigree papers. He opened his van door and called "Come on Elsa". Without any hesitation she jumped in and off they went. I cried myself to sleep that night.

That was the beginning of a very heartbreaking time for me.

The second to go was Kim. He really missed Elsa, as did we all, but we had to find homes for them now, as we'd had enquiries about the property and it seemed like they were very interested. We explained that, if they bought it, they would have to give us time to find homes for the animals, but they were also animal lovers. "If there's any you can't find homes for", they said, "just leave them, we'll have them".

My husband was coming home from work a couple of nights later, when he saw a German Shepherd standing at the gate of other English migrants who had eight acres of land. That would be a good home for Kim, he remembered thinking, if they didn't already have a dog, when a couple of nights later, they pulled up in their station wagon. "We hear you have a dog you're trying to find a good home for. Ours got killed on the road last night and the children are distraught, so we need to get another as soon as possible, one that is good with children". Already the two girls aged about seven and ten years were playing with Kim with his ball and he was in his element. Someone to play with - his dream come true!

The parents loved him on sight. "Could we take him now?" they asked. "Yes", I said. It's no good delaying the inevitable!

They were all so happy, Kim barking in excitement, with his new found little friends. "Come on Kim!" they called, holding open the car door and in he jumped and away they went, promising to let us know how he settled. I had a little weep but my husband was awfully quiet.

"What's wrong, don't you feel happy about them?" "Oh yes", he said "but I feel so guilty". It was then he told me about what he'd thought, "I feel as if just by thinking it, I caused the dog's death". "Don't be silly", I said, "you don't have that much power, anyway it's good Kim is able to help heal the hurt and, knowing Kim, he'll keep them busy". He would play all day if you have the time and he'd never lost his love of life and his amazing sense of fun and he had a heart like Duke's. He'd give those children all the love they could hold.

They kept in touch, they assured us he'd settled in fine, slept in the girls' bedroom and went with them wherever they went, so again I thanked God, for another good home.

Ross and Zeena said we could keep Duke till it got nearer to leaving. The people had decided they wanted to buy the property, so we had agreed to sell. We'd advertised the horses for sale, but on condition they kept the horses together, as they had never been separated and it was going to be bad enough for them leaving the only home the foals had ever known. We had enquiries, but people only wanting one or two of them, but I refused to sell, 'til one day the man who had bought Butcher's property came to see me. The only time I had spoken to him was one day I was trying to sponge mite fluid into Tania's mane and tail and she wouldn't stand still as she hated getting wet, even when it rained. No matter where you happened to be with her, she'd head for home and straight under shelter. So

I was having difficulty trying to persuade her to stand, when this voice behind me said "Would you like a hand with that?" I turned and realised I was by now at the gate and this young man sat astride his horse had been watching me. "Oh! Yes", I said, "I can't get her to stand".

He got off his horse and strolled over. One thing struck me about him; he seemed to move in such a relaxed manner. There was something about him that gave you a sense of confidence and Tania sensed it straight away for, as he reached for the head stall, she became as quiet as a lamb and stood stock still while he sponged her down (I could have killed her). As he sponged, he spoke to her, very gently and softly and

she was putty in his hands. I had noticed this same power if you can call it that, in Kenny. Not a dominating power but a kind of hypnotic draw that animals seem to recognise and thoroughly trust. I have read that American Indians have this gift, especially with horses.
Anyway, he called one day, he said he had heard we were selling the horses. "Yes", I said, "but not separately, the three together or not at all". "Well", he said, "could you and your husband spare a minute, come up to my place, I'd like to show you something".

So we went to his property to see what was so interesting. He went to a stable and walked out with one of the most beautiful horses I've ever seen. "He's lovely," I said. "Yes, he's an American quarter horse", he said, "we are a syndicate who have just had him brought over from America, they are bred for quarter mile races, we are hoping to rear the first Australian quarter horse, but first we have to find good mares to breed from, they have to be good enough to be passed by Gatton Agricultural College and we think your horses are the best we've seen yet and if you'll agree we will get someone out to inspect them". "Okay", I said, "but only on the understanding they are kept together". "They'll be kept here and bred with from here", he promised.

One morning I awoke to the dogs barking furiously from the laundry. I looked out and there was Vic (as we learnt his name) leading round the horses and men with clipboards walking around examining them. I went out, "I hope you don't mind" he said, "these are the men from the Agricultural College". "I guessed so", I said. He introduced me. "Well", they said, "they certainly are the best we've seen yet, although we have a few more to see, we are very impressed with yours, but we'll have to get back to you". This statement worried me a little, as time was now the most crucial factor of all. We had agreed to sell the property and had given a date when we would vacate. The time was approaching when we would have to book our passage home, then there would be no turning back.

Vic said "Please give me a little time, I'm sure they'll be accepted, the syndicate's very impressed".

So we agreed and kept our fingers crossed.

We managed to find a home for everything but Suzy the goat and Winky the cat, but as the people who were buying had fallen in love with her on sight and had made a great fuss of Winky, I knew they wouldn't be a problem.

CHAPTER EIGHT

Time seemed to fly the last few weeks, we'd booked on the "Britanis", another of Chandris Lines' ships and we had arranged to stay with Les and Jean for a week in Sydney before the ship sailed. Sid wanted to take a cine film of the animals and property before we left. "Please don't," I said, "we'll be taking our hurt with us". I didn't think I could ever bear to look at it anyway, but it is something I have come to regret over the years.

A week before we were due to leave, the horses were still in the paddocks and Vic was still waiting for the verdict for Gatton. "Look! Please trust me, I'll buy them, I'll give you the cheque now and whatever happens, you know I'll take good care of them". "Okay", we said, as by now we had very little choice. "I'll collect them tomorrow then". "Please no" I said, "could you leave them in the paddock till we've left, maybe collect them the next day", as I couldn't bear to see them being herded away, confused and wondering what was going on. "Alright" he said, writing out the cheque and handing it over. That was it, all our bridges were burned
.
The new owners were moving in the day after we left, they were thrilled to have the goat and cat and the little boy about five miles bush, took Bluey, the budgie. The last I saw of him, what a picture, the little boy was riding his pony, carrying Bluey in his cage, who was happily singing away, the last of my most cherished pets.

We had sold the house "as is"; this includes the furniture and everything else you choose to leave, so we only packed the necessary items, things we knew we would need and the things of sentimental value. The most important was my husband's tools of trade; he had one large packing case just for these alone, another for clothes and another for household goods. These had to be at the docks five days before the ship sailed.

So the day came, everything was packed and stacked on the trailer behind the car, already to leave. We went to say goodbye to the animals. I'm sure Belle knew something was amiss, as she looked at me with her big sad eyes, as if to say, "I know you wouldn't be doing this if you didn't have to". I gave her a hug and whispered "I'm so sorry", tears rolling down my cheeks.

The foals came prancing over, wondering what was going on. I loved them, said a quiet goodbye and prayed to God they would always be well cared for whatever happened. I hugged Suzy, my funny little friend; she nuzzled me, as if she also knew this was goodbye. Winky wasn't around to say goodbye, but I'm sure cats sense more what's going on. I'd given her a lot of love and attention over the last week, so I think she'd crept off rather than say goodbye. As we drove out of the gate, I had one last look, the horses were munching away in the morning sunshine, and the Kookaburras were calling in the trees. I felt such sadness in my heart, but I thanked God for giving me the time I'd had in my bushland setting home, with all my lovely animals.

I don't remember much of the time before the ship sailed; I do remember Les and Jean begging us not to go. Les even offered Sid half of his garage businesses free, if we'd only stay, but we had made up our minds. My health was more important than anything else was. It was obvious the climate didn't suit me and I knew deep inside I would always be homesick.

The day the ship was due to sail, Les, Jean, Dawn, Kevin & Lesley came to see us off, they were allowed aboard till 1 hour before it sailed. We found our cabin, two berth this time, stacked our cases, then went on deck. I was hard waiting to sail, as you can't help wondering if you've done the right thing. Les and Jean kept saying, "you've still time to change your minds", but we'd made our decision and we'd stick to it.

So the message came over the tannoy, "will all visitors please leave the ship". This was it, we kissed them all goodbye, all of us in tears, promising to write, never to lose touch. They left and in no time at all it was time to sail, three blasts on the funnel and off we slowly sailed from Sydney harbour. I looked up at the bridge, the same bridge that had welcomed me seven years ago.

Now it seemed to be saying a fond farewell. I looked over the harbour and whispered "thank you Australia for being so good to me, I really am sorry to be leaving you, I will always have a place for you in my heart, no matter where I go, you took me to your bosom and made me a beautiful foster home, but now I have to return to my true home, but thank you, I will never forget you.

Goodbye sweet country.

Printed in Great Britain
by Amazon